T0149437

THE ROOSTER
AND
THE HEN

THE ROOSTER
— AND —
THE HEN

THE STORY OF LOVE AT LAST LOOK

DEJI BADIRU

iUniverse books may be ordered through booksellers or by contacting:

iUniverse
1663 Liberty Drive
Bloomington, IN 47403
www.iuniverse.com
1-800-Authors (1-800-288-4677)

ISBN: 978-1-5320-5786-1 (sc)
ISBN: 978-1-5320-5787-8 (e)

Library of Congress Control Number: 2018910862

Print information available on the last page.

iUniverse rev. date: 09/14/2018

ABICS Publications

A Division of
AB International Consulting Services

Books in the ABICS Publications Book Series
(www.abicspublications.com)

The Rooster and the Hen: The Story of Love at Last Look

Kitchen Physics: Dynamic Nigerian Recipes

The Story of Saint Finbarr's College: Contributions to Education and Sports Development in Nigeria

Physics of Soccer II: Science and Strategies for a Better Game

Kitchen Dynamics: The rice way

Consumer Economics: The value of dollars and sense for money management

Youth Soccer Training Slides: A Math and Science Approach

My Little Blue Book of Project Management

8 by 3 Paradigm for Time Management

Badiru's Equation of Student Success: Intelligence, Common Sense, and Self-discipline

Isi Cookbook: Collection of Easy Nigerian Recipes

Blessings of a Father: Education contributions of Father Slattery at Saint Finbarr's College

Physics in the Nigerian Kitchen: The Science, the Art, and the Recipes

The Physics of Soccer: Using Math and Science to Improve Your Game

Getting things done through project management

DEDICATION

To love unfettered through the ages

ACKNOWLEDGMENTS

I THANK AND ACKNOWLEDGE the contributions of Jinan Andrews, Bimbo Orikogbo, and Luke Farrell, whose inquiring young minds, during an informal lunch conversation, posed the question that led me to the need to write this storied documentation.

CHAPTER

1

Genesis of The Story

THIS IS A STORY of love not at first sight. Rather, it is a story of love at last look. If that gets you curious, please read on. I have told the story to friends, family, colleagues, and so on, so much so that it has almost become one of the famed "Deji-Vu, all over again" exposés. Deji-Vu is a play on words by one of my professional colleagues in relation to Yogi Berra's quote of "It is déjà vu all over again." Of course, for the French-speaking aficionados, "déjà vu" means "already seen before." Thus, my repeated stories become "déji-vu" by Deji Badiru.

Why have I repeated the same story so many times, apart from it being an intriguing story? It is because the question always comes up, fueled by general chit-chat tidbits of social conversations. The question often comes in two modes.

One scenario is when someone asks me "where did you and your wife meet?" or another related question along that line. This is a typical nosy question in the American culture. You don't typically find such a question in the Nigerian Yoruba culture, particularly

1

coming from a younger person to a much older person. In the American culture, any young person of any age can ask any older person of any age that question. A direct answer to the question is readily provided by an American. In the traditional (now dying culture) of Yoruba, a young one dare not ask an adult that kind of question. The question would probably attract responses such as "How dare you?" "What an insult?" "Why is that any of your business?" "What has that got to do with your school work?" "Even your father won't ask me that kind of question." In the long-gone practice of the elders, the question could even attract a quick slap, smack, or whack to ensure that such a question never comes up again. It is unfortunate that such a discouraging practice ever existed. It is because of it that many grown Yoruba adults never can answer basic questions about their parents. In the bygone Yoruba days, questions such as "what is your father's age?" or "where was your mother born" or "what is your father's middle name" are often answered with "I don't know." This is not due to being evasive, it is simply due to not knowing for sure because the questions were never raised and addressed within the strict deference culture of the traditional Yoruba family. Anyway, in my own Americanized culture, I always take delight in answering the question in detail regardless of the age, grade, or creed of the person posing the question.

The other scenario is when someone makes a comment about any of my paintings. It doesn't matter which painting. My answer always drifts to "my best painting ever." The comparative quality of any other painting doesn't matter. My best and favorite painting has the best intriguing story that I take delight in re-telling again and again.

So, what is the current story? Please hold your horses, we will get there soon.

CHAPTER

2

The Final Draw

WE ARE GETTING CLOSER to the story. As mentioned before, I have told this story many times in the past, but never documented it in writing. This chapter narrates how the final draw for writing the story came about as a documentation for posterity.

The impetus happened during an informal lunch conversation with a trio of new students at the Air Force Institute of Technology (AFIT) in Dayton, Ohio. At this point, since I mention students, you might wonder what do students have to do with the story. So, I digress temporarily to tell you about my background relative to the student conversation. At the time of this writing, I am the Dean and Senior Academic Officer of the Graduate School of Engineering and Management at the Air Force Institute of Technology and also a Professor of Systems Engineering. I have oversight for planning, directing, and controlling operations related to granting doctoral and master's degrees, professional continuing cyber education, and research and development programs for the US Air Force. I was previously Professor and

Head of Systems Engineering and Management at AFIT, Professor and Department Head of Industrial & Information Engineering at the University of Tennessee, Knoxville, and Professor of Industrial Engineering and Dean of University College at the University of Oklahoma, Norman. I am a registered professional engineer (PE), a certified Project Management Professional (PMP), a Fellow of the Institute of Industrial & Systems Engineers, and a Fellow of the Nigerian Academy of Engineering. I have a BS degree in Industrial Engineering, MS in Mathematics, and MS in Industrial Engineering from Tennessee Technological University, and a Ph.D. degree in Industrial Engineering from the University of Central Florida. So, I have had a substantive instructional, mentoring, and advisory interactions with students over the years. I have diverse areas of avocation. My career and professional pursuits are coupled with my passion for writing about everyday events and interpersonal issues, especially those dealing with social responsibility. Outside of the academic realm, I write motivational poems, editorials, and newspaper commentaries; as well as engaging in paintings and crafts.

It is in the above context that I have a lot of formal and informal conversations with students at all levels at different institutions. So it was that on Friday, August 10th, 2018, I hosted a lunch meeting with Jinan Andrews, Bimbo Orikogbo, and Luke Farrell at my favorite ethnic restaurant, Linh's Bistro (Vietnamese Restaurant) in the vicinity of Wright-Patterson Air Force Base in Dayton, Ohio. All three were new students to AFIT. Jinan and Luke have been assigned to me as interim research assistants for the weeks before classes would start on October 1, 2018. Bimbo was assigned to work as a library assistant at the AFIT library during the period. Although not assigned to work with me, Bimbo was Jinan's friend and, thus, earned the right to attend my group's lunch meeting. Besides, Bimbo is the daughter of an extended family friend (in the Nigerian tradition). They were all graduates (as second lieutenants) of the US Air Force Academy (USAFA) in Colorado Springs, Colorado, which is technically the US Air Force undergraduate school. AFIT is technically the US Air Force graduate school. USAFA graduates coming direct to AFIT for graduate school are referred to as "direct ascension" students, who go on to graduate school without an intervening service assignment. They get their first real service assignment after graduating from AFIT. If the students show up at AFIT before classes start, they are put in what officials call "casual status," which is not my favorite term. I prefer calling them "incoming students" or "early arrivals." During the casual status, the new students, being full-time employees of the Air Force, must be placed on some sort of full-time work assignments at AFIT. This is how it happened that Jinan and Luke were assigned to work with me, since their graduate studies would be in systems engineering, my own area of specialization at AFIT. Don't worry, I will get to the real story soon. Remember, you are supposed to still be holding your horses at this point.

It is my common practice with all those working with me, regardless of how short or long it would be or the type of work, to provide me with their detailed resumes (curricular vitae). Some find this request amusing because they are not applying for a job with me, but they always comply, because I always insist. After learning much about them from the resumes, I often have informal meetings with them to discuss how their interests, experience, expertise, and avocation might align with mine. I always tell them that the more we overlap on general interests, the better we could work together professionally.

Through the resumes and conversations, I learned that Jinan was an expert swimmer and had been the captain of the USAFA swim team. Luke's family was originally from Liverpool, England and he had gone to Russia to watch the 2018 FIFA Soccer World Cup. Bimbo was an avid rock climber and had been a paratrooper (military parachutists) at USAFA. So, we had a lot of common items of interest to talk about.

At the lunch meeting, I ordered my usual, Basil Chicken with an extra-extra helping of steamed rice, which I jokingly refer to as white rice unpolluted and unadulterated. The young ones ask

5

questions that adults take for granted. At some point during the lunch conversation, Jinan asked, "how did you and your wife meet?" That question was precipitated by a preceding question regarding how long my wife and I had been married. I was telling the lunch party about my forthcoming travel in September. I proudly told them about our typical annual routine of celebrating our anniversary by traveling overseas to coincide with the anniversary date. I recounted the recent trips to New York City, Rome, Paris, London, Tokyo, Beijing, and Madrid. It would be Washington, DC in 2018, I announced. "That's cool" one "kid" remarked. Yes, I sometimes teasingly refer to my young students as kids, though they are not exactly kids in the usual sense. They are typically in their twenties in age. But that doesn't matter. At the age of 66, I believe I have earned the right to reaffirm my degree of age separation from the young ones by adoringly referring to them as "kids." Many of them actually enjoy that reference because they see me as some grandfatherly benefactor. The rattling off of the recent anniversary destinations impressed my audience. Someone else (it could have been the same kid) asked me how many such travels so far. "We only started this a few years ago with the New York City travel," I responded in a muted tone. I then followed with "We have been married now for 42 years; it will be 43 next month." "Wow, that's impressive," resorted someone. "Yes, I affirmed," This was immediately followed by the question de jour mentioned earlier. "How did you and your wife meet?", Jinan reiterated. Although I could feel the excitement of responding fully to the question, I playfully played hard to get. She repeated the question. I responded, "it is a long story." I thought that would end that trail of the conversation and veer us off on to another theme. Alas, I misjudged. Instead of dropping the question, she said "We have some time," she reassured me, taking a quick glance at the time (on the cell phone, of course). What nerve! To question me like that when it was obvious I wasn't interested in cooperating. "It is a long story," I warned again, looking at my own watch (analog dial, of course). At that point, all three of them looked at me longingly, waiting for the start of the story. I pretended to be distracted by scooping and forcing a large fork-full of steamed rice into my month. That should put a stop to the expectant stares. After all, these junior officers would not expect the Dean to start speaking with his month full. But, unfortunately, the staring continued, as if the students were practicing a magical stare to elicit my response to the question. The question has been posed and they expected an answer. Lunch period was running out. I would either have to cave in or develop another ploy to fend off the question. There was no escape. I had heightened their expectation by hinting that there was some juicy story to answer the question. I have always taken delight in telling the story. Why now am I vacillating in coming forth with the answer. The story always sends my heart aflutter . . . with excitement. But this time, I could not immediately bring myself to start the story. I suspect it was due to some subconscious reservation. These are new students. I am not close to them socially. There is much gap between our ranks. It was none of their business to know how I met my wife. Overt socializing across the ranks is not particularly endorsed by the military. I wrestled with the decision. To tell or not to tell the story here and now, that's the question. I wondered if they had heard something from my office colleagues about the famous story, thereby creating a tantalizing anticipation of being in the know, like everyone else. Would I be disappointing them by preventing them from being in the know? All these thoughts flashed fast and overlappingly in my mind. We are running out of lunch-time period. The foot-dragging on starting the story could have been due, subconsciously on my part, to the fact that it is, indeed, a long story, for which I would not have time to tell satisfactorily over a confined lunch period. I smiled at the students, as if to say I am satisfied at the consideration, but I am not telling you the story today. Instead of discouraging them, the smile only intensified their curiosity. The staring continued. "Please tell us the story, we want to hear it," they choreographically pleaded. "So, how did you and your wife meet?" Jinan asked again, as if I had ADD (attention deficit disorder) and I needed to be reminded. "It was at work." I said quietly, even though the response rang loudly in their attentive ears. They all leaned forward across the lunch table, as if trying to catch every snippet of the story while fencing off the hearing of other lunch groups. I wasn't exactly whispering, but they leaned forward nonetheless. I leaned back and exhaled. This brought a look of satisfying anticipation to their faces. I could see now that I could not hold back any longer. I have been cornered with nowhere to escape. The story must be told right here and now.

CHAPTER

3

The Story Behind the Story

"How did you and your wife meet?" Jinan asked.

"It was at work in the December timeframe in 1973 in Lagos, Nigeria." I commenced the story, much to the delight of the students.

"Have you seen any of my paintings?" I asked the students.

"No!" They responded in unison.

"Well, I have to show you." I confided.

They looked disappointed. After all, they were spoiling for a juicy story, not a painting-gallery viewing at a lunch table. At this chronological stage in my relationship with the students, they have built up the confidence that I was an approachable senior administrator. I do, indeed, had and still have, what I describe as integrative and inclusive leadership style. I maintain an open-door policy to encourage faculty, staff, administrators, and students to schedule flexible times with me for work-related and general-mentoring purposes. Many, including several students, frequently take me up on the offer. Even though the students have only worked with me for one week, they had already learned my access philosophy around the office. So, they were not bashful in posing questions to me, with proper military respect and protocol, of course. The power structure and reporting hierarchy are upheld in an atmosphere of open and interactive communication.

With my conviction that the students weren't being disrespectful, I quietly pulled out my wireless cell phone and navigated to my family website, www.badiru.com, and linked to the icon for "Deji's Painting Gallery." The first painting on display was the painting of a colorful rooster, proudly crowing, and a beautiful hen, gently pecking. The students were visibly impressed. They leaned forward toward the screen of the phone as if to engage physically with the displayed image, and uttered comments of admiration. "That is great!" "You are such a great artist." "Wow, you painted that?" After all the congratulatory accolades waned, I pointed a finger to the rooster painting and said, "That's the painting that got me my wife." That cracked up the students. Laughter, laughter, laugher. Laughter so loud they could not be muffled by discrete covering of the mouth. In a damped tone, one of the students joked,

"You won your wife in a painting contest?"

I responded, "Sort of, but not quite."

"So, what is the story?"

We will get there in a moment. But first, we need to visit the background of how the painting in question came to materialize.

Early in my youth, I had a flare for artistic pursuits. Even before starting school, I was reported to have a knack for sketching things out on paper, dirt floor, or whatever else happened to be within my vicinity. Everyone expected me to grow up to be a professional artist. By the time I started high school at Saint Finbarr's College, Akoka, Yaba, Lagos, Nigeria, I had already established a reputation of being a fun artist, but without a deep skill that would qualify me as a talented artist. I dabbled in drawing, sketching, and painting, but never seriously contemplated being an artist. I re-drew colorful action-packed covers of comic magazines of the mid-1960s to the delight of family members, school mates, and neighbors. With a carefree attitude of a typical teenager, I did not give much consideration to what I would grow up to be. I just drew pictures for my own enjoyment and satisfaction of just being artistic.

Fortunately, at Saint Finbarr's College, there was a well-equipped Fine Art option, which I enrolled in. I did well in my art classes. The art instructor saw a future artist in me and attempted to veer me in the direction of that profession. For me, it was too early to decide and I was not concerned about committing to one line of career or another. Fortunately, I did well in other core subjects too, including Mathematics, English Language, French, Physics, Chemistry, and Biology. The instructors in every one of those subjects tried to win me over to their own career paths. I was nonchalant about any one of the areas. My all-around good performance in all my high school subjects eventually earned me a Grade I Distinction in the West African School Certificate (WASC) external examination when I graduated from Saint Finbarr's College in December 1972.

That I met and married my wife was due to an act of coincidence that had its roots in the Art Room of Saint Finbarr's College. Had I not attended Saint Finbarr's College; had I not been in the school's art room painting a colorful rooster; had I not been in good favour with the art teacher; had the art teacher not given me a job referral to Mr. Nupo Samuel at the Lagos State Ministry of Education – Audio Visual Aids Section; had I not returned to the painting of the colorful rooster; I would not have my wife of today. It was a step-wise progression from Saint Finbarr's College art room to the eventual liaison with my future wife.

I was a good student of art and our art teacher took a special interest in my future professional outlook. He felt that I was good enough to become a renowned professional artist. Being somewhat of an all-rounder, each of my other teachers had expressed similar expectations that I would go into a profession fitting his or her own subject. The French teacher, Mr. Akinrimade, expected me to become a professional in the Nigerian foreign mission with assignments to French-speaking countries. He later tried to get me to attend the Nigerian Defense Academy (NDA), thinking that I would make a great Army officer in Nigeria's missions in the African Francophone countries. The Biology teacher, Mr. A. A. Kpotie, who later became principal, advised that I should go into the medical field. The English teacher hoped that I would follow his profession and become an English teacher, or a writer, or a poet. The physics teacher suggested that I would make an excellent scientist. My Mathematics teacher wanted me to become an engineer. Observing my later performance in his own Religious Studies class, Father himself thought I would be a good religious ambassador, bridging the division between Christians and Moslems. As for me, I just went with the flow. I did not pay much attention to what the future held for me in terms of a profession. I believed in existentialism and adapted to whatever came up for the moment. Enjoying the moment was all that mattered to me.

In the Art room, I experimented with various drawing and painting exercises. It was in preparation for my Art School Certificate examination that I came across the painting of animals. The painting of one particular colorful rooster (cock) attracted my attention for several weeks. I never completed the painting to my own level of satisfaction. So, I abandoned the project. This was around the middle of 1972. A couple of years later, it turned out that a return to the painting of a colorful rooster would seal my fate with my future wife.

Two weeks after finishing my School Certificate examination I secured a job as a factory supervisor at Associated Industries Limited (AIL) in Ikeja. My School Cert results had not come out by that time. So, I did not know what direction I was going to pursue either in terms of further studies or long-term employment. I was on night shift at AIL, starting work around 3p.m. and closing at 11p.m. I never enjoyed the work at all, even though the salary was very good by the standards of the day. I longed for a "more regular" job schedule, where I would close around 4 p.m. and I could spend the afternoons and evenings with my neighbourhood friends. So, I abruptly left AIL after only three weeks. My next employment was at Union Trading Company (UTC) as an Accounts Clerk at the Broad Street location of the company. I did well at this job, but the work schedule was too oppressive for a freshly-liberated high school graduate whose primary interest was having afternoon fun in the neighbourhood. As an Accounts Clerk, I was required to work overtime sometimes in the evenings and weekends. This did not suit me well. So, I left UTC after two months, although I had no immediate prospects for another employment. Unemployed, I roamed the streets of Lagos as I had been accustomed to in search of new friendships and fun opportunities. I greatly enjoyed the freedom and the absence of worries of those days. I enjoyed the freedom to roam the city. Even nowadays, I still enjoy my hands-on and legs-on approach to duties. "Legs-on" means that I like going places to get things done directly myself. This direct approach is a good way to ensure efficiency and effectiveness of actions. In fact, the lunch outing with my new students was a part of my legs-on outing to get to know the students better and for them to know me better, to create a better working relationship . . . for the sake of efficiency, effectiveness, and productivity.

By March 1973, the School Cert results were out and Father Slattery had personally sent someone to my residence at 13 Brickfield Road, Apapa Road to proudly announce that I came out with Grade I Distinction in the School Cert. This energized me to want to drop my unemployment status. So, I went back to the job market in search of re-employment. Heartened by my School Cert results, I was not concerned about not being successful in the job market. My most cherished results were a "1" in English, a "1" in French, a "2" in Mathematics, and a "2" in Art. Although I did well in all my subjects, these were my four favorite and preferred subjects.

My former Art teacher at Saint Finbarr's College came to know of how well I had performed in the School Certificate Art examination and decided that he must get me into the art profession. He sent a message to me at home to inform me that the Lagos State Ministry of Education's Audio Visual Aids Section on Broad Street was in need of a graphics artist. He referred me to a friend of his, Mr. S. Nupo Samuel, who was a senior staff in charge of the Art Unit. Mr. Samuel received his BSc in Fine Art from Ahmadu Bello University. He would later encourage me to seek admission for Fine Art at the same university. I spent several weeks doing gratis drawing for Mr. Samuel in anticipation of an appropriate job opening in the Art Unit. He implored me to be patient. He had to find the right time and occasion to introduce me to his boss, the head of the Audio Visual Aids Section. The Section Head at that time was Mrs. F. R. A. Thanni. She had informed Mr. Samuel that the section did not have any graphics artist positions even though Mr. Samuel urgently needed an assistant. But after several weeks of drawing for the Section free of charge, Mrs. Thanni decided, upon becoming aware of my School Cert results, that she could get me into the Ministry as a Clerical Officer. That was how I started as a Clerical Officer in the Lagos State Ministry of Education in April 1973. I was immediately posted to the Audio Visual Aids Section. Although my official title was Clerical Officer, my actual duties were as a graphics artist. I drew pictures that accompanied English language captions for children's television programs. The programs were designed to introduce children to the English Language. If a caption said, "This is a dog," I would draw a dog to depict the context. It was a fun and rewarding job. The workload was very low because we broadcasted the programs only once a week. So, in-between official drawing assignments, I would engage in casual drawing and painting.

4

The Story of the Rooster and the Hen

THE FULL BACKGROUND OF the story is now set. So, back to the question of "How did you and your wife meet?"

In early December 1973, Miss Iswat Kuforiji, was employed in the same Audio Visual Aids Section. I immediately set my eyes on her as my future wife. I was only 21 and she was only 17. But I was undeterred by our youthful ages. She was very beautiful and unattached. She had just moved to Lagos from Ilaro, a much smaller town than Lagos. In fact, Ilaro was a village in comparison to the "megapulous" attributes of the city of Lagos. I was determined to snatch her before she could fall into the hands of Lagos boys with roving eyes.

Finbarr's boys were brash and self-assured. The belief was that every girl in Lagos wanted to know and date Finbarr's boys. Obviously, no one gave Iswat a pre-brief about this before she came to Lagos.

So, I knew I had to move fast to protect her from the likes of me. I began to direct all my attention and energy to convincing her that I was the designated person for her. Unfortunately, all my attempts to woo her were futile. She clearly hated my guts. She detested my Lagos-boy arrogance. The air of city sophistication that I had tried to use to impress her actually turned her against me. She would have nothing to do with me. She rebuffed and declined my initial attempts to strike up a conversation. She would, in later years, say that a woman should never be an easy catch. Even my proud Saint Finbarr's College roots could not immediately do the trick. The Boys of Saint Finbarr's College in those days believed in and used the aura of Saint Finbarr's College to get girls. Many high-school girls in Lagos at that time were anxious to fall for a Finbarr's boy. But this girl, coming from the relatively rural setting of Ilaro, was not aware of the Saint Finbarr's College aura. So, she was not impressed. I decided to give up on her because, frankly, there were other older fishes already in the catch. I was on the verge of telling her off when my Saint Finbarr's College origin came into place in a very unexpected way.

Since she was not responding, I had redirected my attention once again to my casual drawings and paintings in the office. I returned to the painting of the colorful rooster that I had abandoned in the Saint Finbarr's College Art Room several months earlier. One day, I was seriously engrossed in painting the rooster when Iswat came beside me to ask what I was painting.

A stroke of ingenuity struck me right then. Without time to think of a cute response, I blurted out "This colorful rooster that I am painting represents me; and right here beside him I am going to paint a hen; and that hen will represent you."

Well, that did the trick. She was completely disarmed. She was dumbfounded by the quip. All she could mutter was, "Okay." And that was how we embarked on our journey of dating and eventually getting married in 1975. The painting was subsequently completed, but not on the schedule I had originally planned. Having secured her attention, I maintained a leisurely schedule of returning to the painting and finessing the rooster and the hen. I signed the painting for July 1973, which signified when I returned seriously to the painting. Not recalling when I actually finished the painting, I opted to use the starting date of July 1973. I actually never finished the painting for many years because for several months after we started dating, I took delight in returning to the painting to add another stroke of excellence to the rooster-and-the-hen rendition.

September 25, 2017 marked our 42nd wedding anniversary. To this date, the 1973 painting of the rooster and the hen has remained a favorite feature of our home decoration and office conversation.

When I came to the USA for further studies in December 1975, I brought the painting with me as my most-priced possession. The photograph of the painting is used for the cover of this book.

Therein lies the much-awaited story.

Jinan, Bimbo, and Luke are now in the know, just like everyone else. The question has been answered and everyone is now satisfied. But Jinan wasn't done with her inquiring mind.

She commented: "I am surprised you have not written a book about that story."

I promised her that I would add it to my list of writing chores. That formed the motivation and impetus for this book. Now that the book has been written, I may not have to answer the question directly again. I may just point any new inquiring mind to go and read the book.

The photograph below is from our early album from our dating days.

5

My Background from
Saint Finbarr's College

ANY STORY OF MINE will not be complete without the concomitant story of Saint Finbarr's College. My life is intertwined with the story of Saint Finbarr's College. There are schools and then there are schools, but there is no school like Saint Finbarr's College, Akoka, Yaba, Lagos, Nigeria. This book is the third in my books on Saint Finbarr's College and the monumental contributions of Reverend Father Denis Joseph Slattery, SMA, an Irish Priest and a member of Society of African Missions. The **Society of African Missions** (SMA) is a Roman Catholic missionary organization. The society's members come from around the world with a commitment to serve the people of Africa and those of African descent.

Father Slattery came, he saw, and he advanced the nation of Nigeria through his multi-faceted contributions to education, sports, and discipline. His memory can never be allowed to wane in Nigeria. In this regard, this book, **The Story of Saint Finbarr's**

College, documents the continuing efforts of Saint Finbarr's College Old Boys Association (SFCOBA) around the World to enliven the story of the school. This book is written from my own personal first-hand perspective. Similar stories are often told by other ex-students from their own respective perspectives. All stories have the same similar vein, thus, confirming the consistency of the legacy of Father Slattery. You cannot separate the story of Father Slattery from the story of Saint Finbarr's College and vice versa. Both stories go hand-in-hand.

Sorry if you have heard this part of my story before elsewhere, but the stories of Father Slattery and Saint Finbarr's College must be told again and again in all possible avenues. It is, indeed, one of the *"Déji Vu* All Over Again."

The story of Saint Finbarr's College is fascinating and inspiring. The story revolves around the life and deeds of Reverend Denis Joseph Slattery, an Irish Catholic priest, who came to Nigeria in 1941 and never left, until his work was done. "Done" in this sense refers to the completion of planting the seeds of success for his Saint Finbarr's students. Those seeds continue to germinate and bear fruits even after he finally left Nigeria (in forced ministerial retirement in 2000 and his death in 2003. The tentacles of the positive legacies of Father Slattery and Saint Finbarr's College can be seen all over the world today, as graduates of the school continue to make professional inroads on various platforms around the world.

This book represents a textual and pictorial commemoration of the contributions of Father Slattery to education, youth discipline, and sports development in Nigeria. It is designed as an archival reference to many of Finbarr's historical records and accolades.

The history of Saint Finbarr's College is a favorite pastime of all the former and present students of the school. Saint Finbarr's College is most noted for three characteristics:

1. Academics
2. Football
3. Discipline

It was in recognition and appreciation of the impacts of the above attributes of Saint Finbarr's College that I wrote the previous two-book series on Blessings of a Father (2005, 2013).

What I am today, professionally, is the product of the educational and discipline foundations I acquired at Saint Finbarr's College. For this, I remain very grateful. My biographical sketch below (written in third person) sums up the end product of my journey that started at Saint Finbarr's College under the watchful eye and magnanimous deeds of Reverend Father Slattery.

Reverend Father Denis Joseph Slattery came to Nigeria in 1941. Having served in a parish at Ilawe-Ekiti, in the Yoruba Inland Town of Ilawe-Ekiti, in the Old Western Region, Father Slattery was posted to Saint Gregory's College, Obalende as a teacher and later became the Games Master. He later became the editor of the Catholic Herald in Mushin. It was during this period that the thought of establishing a unique school occurred to him. His school became the first bilateral school in the country, combining full Grammar (called Basic) with Arts and Technical subjects. In the 1955/56 academic year, with six students, fondly referred to as "the first six of the first six", a new school, but without a name, was born. The "first six of the first six" refers to the first six students in the first six years of Saint Finbarr's College.

The new school had no address and had to be accommodated in the newly-built St. Paul's Catholic Primary School, Abebe Village, Apapa Road, Ebute-Metta, Lagos.

The next task was to look for a site for the new school. Rev. Father D. J. Slattery, after an eleven-month search, which took him through the then wilderness area of Apapa, now the present location of the National Stadium. Further searches eventually got him to another wilderness area in Akoka, where he met a man who knew Father Slattery, but whom Father Slattery did not know. The friendly disposition of the man made it easy for Father Slattery to acquire a twenty-plot piece of land in the present site of the school. In 1959, the school moved from Apapa Road to its present site in Akoka, and in 1963, the school was officially opened by Dr. Nnamdi

Azikiwe, the first President of Nigeria, who was a personal friend of Father Slattery.

In a tactical move, he got a grant from the then British colonial government, with which he set up a ten-classroom block, two technical drawing rooms, a technical block, an administrative block, which also housed the teachers staff room, and a dining-room assembly hall with a well-equipped kitchen. Among the first teachers of the school were the late Chief Albert Bankole, Father Slattery himself, and Mr. F. Ekpeti.

Although a complete and accurate listing of the first set of students is difficult for me to come by at this time, due to the long passage of time, oral accounts indicate that the first set of students, known as Finbarr's First Set (FFS), included very renowned names in Nigeria.

The first National President of SFCOBA, A. Madufor, came from FFS. The second National President was Tom Borha, an editor of Concord Group of Newspapers. The Third National President was M A C Odu, an Estate Surveyor and Valuer. SFCOBA accomplished a lot of things on behalf of Saint Finbarr's College. Land Surveying was conducted to establish the spatial limits of the school permanently. The order of Distinguished Conquerors (DC) was created to recognize distinguished alumni of the school. Tom Borha received the first one. I received the honor in 1998.

The Presidency of SFCOBA shifted from FFS in 1994 when Segun Ajanlekoko was elected. Segun quickly elevated SFCOBA and SFC into more national and international prominence through a variety of high-profile activities and projects. I met Segun around 1995 and we have both remained staunch advocates for SFC. The system of identifying students by their class years (sets) was established and advanced by SFCOBA. I belong to the 1972 Set.

When Mr. Yinka Bashorun became the national president, he instituted the process of unifying the various branches of SFCOBA domestically and abroad under one National and International SFCOBA. Everyone, to the last man, has been committed to the task of rekindling the glory days of Saint Finbarr's College.

The school made its first attempt at the West African School Certificate Examinations in 1961, having been approved in 1960. In that first attempt, the technical department had 100% passes, with 80% making 3 or 4 credits, while the Grammar, or basic as they were called, had 50% passes with two of them making distinctions. These boys were also tops in sports and Vice-Admiral Patrick Koshoni (Rtd) happens to be one of the two. From then on, the academic results kept improving year after year, with the technical department consistently recording 100% passes. In fact, in those days of Grade 1, Grade 2, and Grade 3 categorization of WAEC results, whenever the result was released, the understanding or common expectation was that all candidates would normally pass and what everybody was interested in was how many came out in Grade One or Grade Two: Grade Three was regarded as a consolation result. This trend remained true until the government takeover of schools in the mid 1970s.

Sports Excellence of Saint Finbarr's College

Rev. Father Denis J. Slattery, being a Games Master and an International Referee, was very eager to put the school at the forefront quickly in football since it would take 5 years for the school to prove its excellence in academics. In its first year of existence, it pitched itself in a football match against its host Primary School, St. Paul's Primary School, Apapa Road and lost 1-2. In 1957, it faced much older St. Gregory's "Rabbits," where Father Slattery himself had been a Games Master. The school later had a number of matches with another older School, the Ahmadiya College, Agege. It was a very ambitious venture for the school, in its first four years of existence on 3rd June 1960, to make its first attempt on the Zard Cup, a nationwide inter-Secondary School competition, which later became the Principals Cup. The school again lost to its counterpart institution, St. Gregory's College, 1-3. In 1961 it met the school again and lost 0-1 after an initial draw of

2-2. In 1962, Saint Finbarr's College won the Principals Cup for the first time, only six years after being established. This victory was repeated in 1966, 1968, and 1969. From then the team from Saint Finbarr's College became the team to beat. Weaker teams feared any match with Saint Finbarr's while stronger ones like C.M.S. Grammar School, Baptist Academy, Igbobi College, and of course, the big brother Saint Gregory's College, always looked forward to a tough encounter. In 1971, 1972, and 1973, the school kept the Principals Cup, having won it three consecutive times.

It is noteworthy that in the 1970s and 1980s the school produced international players such as Thompson Oliha, Nduka Ugbade, Samson SiaSia, and Henry Nwosu, just to mention a few. In fact, in those days, for any candidate to aspire to come to St. Finbarr's, he had to be academically sound and/or physically superior in football. Stephen Keshi, who captained a Finbarr's team, went on to captain and coach national teams.

Rev. Father Denis J. Slattery placed a very high premium on discipline and could expel any student even if he was the best in academics or in football, once it was established that he had committed a serious offense. The gate used to be referred to as the gate of no return. There was no point in appealing a case of expulsion. Father Slattery never entertained such appeals – no pleading, no begging, and no beseeching. Saint Finbarr's College had four commandments, which constitute the Moral Pillars of the school.

(1) Any student caught stealing will be expelled.
(2) Any student caught copying during an examination time will be expelled.
(3) Any student caught leaving the school compound during school hours without the Principal's permission will be expelled.
(4) Any student caught smoking or with drugs will be expelled.

There was no in-between sanctions in the scale of punished. You are either retained or expelled. Period!

By the early 1970s Rev. Fr. D. J. Slattery had a vision of making St. Finbarr's College all-encompassing in technical studies. He, therefore, decided to expand the technical workshops to cater both for the Senior and Junior Student. He introduced auto mechanics, electrical, and electronics departments. Two modern technical workshops were built from grants raised by his friends and overseas associates. The workshops were completed and fully equipped. They had hardly been used for two years when the government took over private schools in 1976. From 1976, the ideals for which Saint Finbarr's College was known, started to decline rapidly. Under government management, the school became over-populated and student indiscipline reigned. The decline reached a frightening level in the second half of the 1990s.

Fortunately, the government eventually deemed it wise to officially relinquish the takeover of private schools on October 2nd, 2001. Thus, Saint Finbarr's College started its second phase of academic advancement, alas without the all-encompassing presence of Father Slattery. By the time the school was returned to the Church, Father Slattery had diverted his attention to other pastoral pursuits. The return of the school took effect in 2003, after much educational damage has been done by the government. A furious academic cleansing ensued and many of the students who could not adjust were dismissed while those who could not stand the changes withdrew voluntarily. Consequently, by 2005, the enrolment at the school has gone down to a manageable level of 658 with the inherited "government students" constituting 413 students of the population. Below is a list of the noted principals of Saint Finbarr's College.

(1) Very Reverend Father Denis J. Slattery, Founding Principal, 1955-1975
(2) Late Anthony Omoera, 1975-1976
(3) Mr. A. A. Kpotie, 1977-1998
(4) Mr. Joseph Adusse, 1998-2001

The school has since been managed by a sequence of administrators from the Catholic Mission. Saint Finbarr's College has spread its tentacles around the world. Several "old boys" of the school are now in key productive and influential positions around the world. Like other notable high schools in Nigeria, Finbarr's has made significant contributions in human resource development in Nigeria. But one distinct and unmistakable fact about Finbarr's is that it has a unifying force -- Rev. Fr. Denis Slattery (even after his death). The man and the name continue to strike a sense of refreshing chill in our hearts.

All graduates of Saint Finbarr's College remain very proud of the school's heritage. Father Slattery encouraged each person to embrace whatever his family religion dictated; but he demanded the study of the Bible as a source of well-rounded education. Thus, Bible Religious Studies was a core subject at the school. Father taught his students to enjoy the thrills and perils of playing sports as a preparation for the other challenges of life. The discipline received from the school has served us very well. It is probably the single most important factor in the professional and personal success of Saint Finbarr's College "Old Boys." In the Yoruba language, Finbarrians are fondly referred to as "Omo Slattery," meaning Slattery's children. Yes, he was our father both in the figurative sense as well as in the spiritual sense.

Father Slattery trained us to be what we are and his lesson still lives on in every one of us. Although his service was primarily in Nigeria, his good example should be publicized to serve other parts of the world. To the last man, every Finbarrian (former and present) has the unity of purpose to disseminate the glory of Saint Finbarr's College, Akoka, Lagos, Nigeria.

St. Finbarr's College was named after Saint Finbarr of Cork City, Ireland. The narrative that follows is based partially on historical recollections of F. Ogundipe and supplemented by other student reports. The first stream of students in the college comprised 68 (sixty-eight) students in two classes of 34 students each. There were only four members of staff in the service of the school. Rev.

Fr. Slattery the principal, two teachers and one office clerk who was a seminarian. Two weeks after resumption from 21st January-10th February the school went on recess on account of the visit of Queen of England and Head of Commonwealth of Nations, who was visiting Nigeria at the time. The whole class of 1956 took part in the events culminating in Youth Day Parade at Race Course, Lagos in honor of the Queen. St. Finbarr's College bore the parade number 162. Classes resumed in the middle of February. Father Slattery himself taught English Language, Literature, Religious Knowledge and Latin. Mr. Bankole, now Chief Bankole taught General Science and Arithmetic, Algebra Geometry and Singing. Mr Ferdinand Ejike taught History and Geography. The first feast of Saint Finbarr, the patron saint of the school, was celebrated on 25th day of September, 1956 with Mass said by Father Slattery, with Openibo, Koshoni Jr and Ogundipe as mass servers.

Early accounts by FFS members indicate that the first interhouse sports festival of the school took place in 1956. That same founding year, SFC participated in Schools Table Tennis Championships with Jamogha, Ayeni and Wilson as Finbarr's stars. The first soccer match was played against host primary school, St. Paul's Primary School. Finbarr's lost 1-2 in an exciting game, which featured Paul Gborjoh alias P J Cobbler. Toward the end of 1956 another encounter was organized with Babies Team of St. Gregory's College, a sister school from where Father Slattery came to found Finbarr's. In 1957, Finbarr's table tennis and soccer teams went over to Abeokuta to play Leonians. Messrs Henry Ekpeti and Ayo Adefolaju and G U M Nwagbara joined the teaching staff. Mr. Ekpeti taught Latin, Mr. Adefolaju taught Mathematics while Nwagbara taught History and Geography. Mr. Onabolu taught Fine Art. In 1958 Mr. Flyn came on staff from Ireland to teach Physics and Chemistry. Mr T C Nwosu, Mr Oweh and Mr. Oguike also joined the teaching staff. In January 1959, students moved to the permanent site at Akoka. The Bursar was Pa Adefuye, Head Laborer was Abu, Head of the new Department of Metalwork was Mr. Mooney. Mr. Flyn assumed Headship of Woodwork Department. Mr. Tommy joined during that year to take over teaching of English Language and Literature from Father Slattery. Mr. Omopariola joined to teach History. From 1960 the complement of staff was enlarged to include Mr. Drumm for Additional Mathematics, Elementary Mathematics and Physics; Mr. Mackenzie for Chemistry; Mr Omopariola for History; Mr. Oguike for Geography. Mr. Oguike left that year for further studies in USA; Mr. Nwagbara, who had left the previous year returned to teach History and Geogrpahy. Mr Nwosu left soon afterwards and Biology fell into the laps of Mr. Okpara before Mr. Nwajei arrived.

Finbarr's entered the Grier Cup competition in 1960. That year, the only qualifier, Eddy Akika, won the coveted Victor Ludorum Trophy winning Hurdles, Long Jump and coming second in High Jump event. Finbarr's entered the Zard Cup on June 2nd, 1960 and lost to St. Gregory's College 1-3. Mr. Drumm was Games Master, Alex Tolefe was Team Manager and Finbarr's Captain was Albert Alotey. On the 19th of June 1961 Finbarr's lost once more to St. Gregory's 0-1 in quarter final of the cup. The same day, Finbarr's was eliminated from the National Table Tennis Championship at Ibadan. Finbarr's lost at Semi Final Match 4-5 to Ansar U Deen College Isolo. Finbarr's stars were Heny Jamogha, Matin Adewusi, and Olusola John.

The first Zard Cup victory came in August 1962 when Finbarr's beat St. Gregorys's College 2-1 after an earlier 2-2 draw under the captainship of Jide Akinosoye (Akinzawelle). It is vital to recall the following : Patrick Koshoni who designed SFC badge unofficially in November 1956 on the blackboard. A proper school badge came in 1957. Jaamogha created the current shape of the badge in 1957 and Father Slattery approved it. Finbarr's lost a student, Pius Okifo, in 1957.

SFC van was purchased in 1959 and sprayed in school colors by Mr. Tommy. Ogundanna, a long-range runner was the first van conductor.

As recollected by many graduates of SFC, tribes and tongues did not make any difference to anyone at Saint Finbarr's then, and they should not make any difference now. Other lists and accounts have been provided by several other Old Boys, including M. A. C. Odu. I did not make an attempt to reconcile the various lists of the First-Six students because, frankly, the lists are from different historical recollections and perspectives of the different early students and should be preserved as such. Even in the Bible, the Gospels by various Prophets are preserved as originally documented. In a non-computer era, all we can do is rely on the personal accounts and recollections of those offering testimonies. The government takeover of SFC probably led to the loss of crucial archival records of the early years of the college. Those records could have helped to authenticate each list.

After all these years, Saint Finbarr's College continues to excel in Academics, Sports, and Discipline. As of the time of this writing (2018), the school continues to receive accolades for its multi-dimensional accomplishments. In 2017, Business Day Research and Intelligence Unit (BRIU) published a guide to the best schools in Lagos, Nigeria. Saint Finbarr's College was listed among the topmost secondary schools in Lagos State. The school's performance in the West African Senior School Certificate Examinations since 2013 have been extraordinary. Based on the number of students who obtained five credits including Mathematics and English Language, the pass rates have been 98.7% in 2013, 100% in 2014, 97.4% in 2015 95%, in 2016 97.4% and 98.2% in 2017. Finbarr's students have been winning laurels at various academic competitions, including Helmbridge, Olympiad, Inter-collegiate Quiz and Debate, and so on.

Please score a checkmark for academics!

In the same vein, Saint Finbarr's College won Soccer Guarantee Trust (GT) Bank Championship on June 29, 2017 at Onikan Stadium, Lagos, Nigeria. The school has expanded its sports excellence to include basketball, tennis, volleyball and, badminton.

Please score a checkmark for sports excellence!

Overall, the virtues of discipline, self-control, respect, care for others, honesty, obedience, hard work, dedication, diligence, and resilience continue to be instilled in Finbarr's students on a daily basis. Thus, Saint Finbarr's College provides holistic education for its students.

In an era when some holy men are charged with doing unholy things, Father Slattery was holy and dedicated to the cause throughout his life of sanctity. There was no flattery or fakery about him.

"Slattery, No Flattery" was a common catchphrase in Lagos, Nigeria about the ways and deeds of Father Slattery. A picture is worth a thousand words. There are not enough words to describe the immense widespread contributions of Reverend Denis Joseph Slattery to education in Nigeria. So, I have generously supplemented words with photographic images of the deeds of Father Slattery. Even after his death since 2003, his deeds continue to influence the lives of those who ever had the good fortune to be associated with Father Slattery either directly or through the continuing legacy of his Saint Finbarr's College, Akoka-Yaba, Lagos, Nigeria.

In the days of Father Slattery, all roads led to Saint Finbarr's College, Akoka, Yaba. All parents in Lagos wished and clamored for their children to go to Saint Finbarr's College, even though there were several other highly-regarded secondary schools in Lagos, including King's College, Igbobi College, Saint Gregory's College, Ansa-ud-deen College, Baptist Academy, and so on. As a high school aspirant in those days, my own initial goal was to attend King's College, until I came across the educational and sports triumphs of Saint Finbarr's College and the personal and direct touch of Father Slattery. It was a dichotomy of a special kind to have a school that excelled in sports (football, i.e., soccer) while simultaneously winning national accolades in educational accomplishments. I was provisionally selected for an interview to enter King's College, but I was utterly devastated when I did not make the cut. By divine intervention, Saint Finbarr's College came along and I was admitted. I was elated. The story of my admission to Saint Finbarr's College is still a fortuitous occurrence that still astonishes me even today. Had I not gained a last-minute admission to Saint Finbarr's during that 1968 admission cycle, it would have been an up-hill challenge, if not an impossible pursuit, during the next annual admissions cycle. I am convinced today that I would not have been any more competitive in 1969 than I was in 1968 in entering a reputable high school in Lagos area. The positive experience of how Saint Finbarr's College came to my academic rescue still determines how I view educational opportunities these days and how I fervently support giving educational opportunities to qualified young minds of today.

Reverend Father Joseph Slattery was born in Fermoy in the County of Cork, South Ireland, on 29th February, 1916, a product of a strong Irish heritage. The Irish are noted for their constant search for self-determination among dominant neighbors. He later became a Catholic priest, founder of Schools, sport administrator, an editor, and a journalist. Father Slattery is a leap-year child. He was always very proud of his leap-year birth date, claiming to be only one-fourth of his actual age. His parents, Mr. Timothy Slattery and Mrs. Kate Slattery (Née Curtin), were blessed with eight children. Denis was the seventh child of the family. Timothy Slattery was a master-cutter and Kate Slattery was a trained dress-maker. They were both from Barrington, Fermoy, a little provincial town in the County of Cork, in the south of Ireland, where the Slattery generations had lived since the 13th century.

The Slattery family was known as "Doers"; a family with a deep sense of adventure, enterprise, and great achievement. The Irish adventurous spirit has remained their greatest contribution to the world. They stride the world in pastoral and political life, breaking new grounds in all spheres.

The American people today remember the Irish among them as the descendants of the builders of Modern America. In 1776, at the signing of the American Constitution, six Irish citizens were signatories to that historic instrument of governance. Timothy Slattery was a disciplinarian, stern, and straight. Kate Slattery was a quiet, serene, and very charitable lady – a combination that was perhaps very necessary for raising eight children, six boys and two girls.

The Slatterys were a family of sportsmen, a trait presumably taken from their father. Timothy Slattery was a great footballer and represented his country as a potential sportsman. His children, particularly Denis, simply carried on the tradition. At a very tender age, Denis J. Slattery was enrolled for his kindergarten education at the Christian Brothers School in Fermoy. He was the only Slattery who did not attend the local Convent school. Young Denis refused to go "to the nuns" at the Presentation Convent. At the Christian Brothers School, the young Slattery was remembered as a wild young man. A healthy kind of wildness, they would say. His activities included *"climbing the highest tree over the River Blackwater and plunging into the deepest depth, searching the woods and forest for birds' nests and eggs, and following the grey hounds on Sunday Soccer."*

He became an Altar boy at the age of ten. He was an excellent liturgist but an average Altar boy. Once an old man who was regular at Mass called him and said, "You serve Mass beautifully. I think you will make a priest." This seemingly harmless remark would come to plant the seed of his vocation. Young Denis had a seriousness of purpose and had often talked about vocations and in due time, he entered the Junior Secondary.

In the Seminary, life was rather drab and hard. Food was poor, dormitories were badly heated, and the chapel was only heated on Sundays. By the second year he had sciatica. He recovered and buried himself deeper into his chosen vocation. He spent two years in the seminary. The extra year was spent getting private tuition in Latin to enable him to pass the Matriculation examination.

The year 1932 marked when Denis Joseph Slattery began his missionary vocation. By 1934, he entered the Novitiate in Clough for a period of two years, and on the 17th December, 1939, he was ordained a priest. He was studious and prayerful at the major Seminary, so he was chosen to go to Rome and study the scriptures in 1940. He was not destined to be in Rome! The 2nd World War broke out and Mussolini shook hands with Hitler, so Rome was out for young Father Denis.

Rev. Father Slattery's first assignment after ordainment was to contribute to raising money for the Church. He felt humiliated because he had to practically beg. Little did he realize that he would be doing the same for the rest of his life. This was the beginning of an arduous and tasking pastoral life. In faraway Lagos, Nigeria, Archbishop Leo Taylor was in dire need of teachers for his diocese. In 1941, the 2nd World War was at its peak. Rev. Fr. Denis Joseph Slattery, 25-year-old Catholic Priest of the Society of African Missions (SMA), was on his way to his posting in Africa. This young Irish priest was part of a growing Irish spiritual empire that included China and the Philippines. The trip was punctuated by a German air attack on the convoy. A German plane had dropped 3 bombs on their ship, which was sailing from Glasgow in a convoy of 50 ships carrying Allied Forces on the Atlantic Ocean. In the tremor following the bombing, the ship rocked violently, dipping from left to right, but did not sink. When they finally sailed into Lagos, the Germans were presumably bombing the Lagos port and ships were not berthing. The ship headed for Port-Harcourt where she berthed. The journey was continued by train from Port-Harcourt to Kaduna to Lagos.

Lagos in 1941 had its fascination for the young Irishman. This is the white man's grave, he wondered. But he did not reckon with Ilawe-Ekiti, a little village in the hinterland of the Western part of Nigeria. Archbishop Taylor was waiting in Lagos. He would welcome the young priest and send him to Ilawe-Ekiti. On his first night at Ilawe-Ekiti, young Fr. Slattery was confronted by a strange pastoral duty. At midnight, a black face had poked its head into the house to ask the Rev. Father to come immediately and give blessing to a dying Christian. He performed his pastoral duties, but the picture remained with him; the black face and the black night.

By the 1940s Archbishop Leo Taylor had built a strong missionary base in the Lagos Diocese. Well-respected and loved by many, Archbishop Taylor was a member of the Society of African Missions (SMA) and of course, the quintessential missionary. He was to recall Rev. Fr. Slattery to Lagos in 1942. By now the young priest he sent to Ilawe-Ekiti now spoke the Yoruba language and could give confession in the language. In Lagos, he was posted to St. Gregory's College, Obalende, as a teacher and games master. His stature seemed to have endeared him to his new students. A mutual relationship was formed which led to great exploits in the football field. The stay at St. Gregory's College was short.

In 1943, he was posted to the Catholic Printing Press as journalist and later Editor of *Catholic Herald.* At the Herald he cultivated a radical posture and became concerned about Nigeria's self-determination as he thundered from the newspaper and the pulpit, "Nigeria for Nigerians." His years as Editor of the Catholic Herald were turbulent. Through the paper, he contributed to the pre-independence struggle, forming a lasting relationship with Labour leaders and politicians. He used the Herald to champion the workers' cause during the general strike of 1945 and the Enugu Coal Mine strike where twenty striking miners were killed. Thrice, the British Colonial Government tried to throw him out of the country, after several warnings. But according to him he was just doing his duty. ***"The British are gone and I (Slattery) am still here,"*** Slattery would later boast. Fr. Slattery later went on to write his Masters thesis on the labour struggle in Nigeria. A founding member of the Nigerian Union of Journalists (NUJ) and the Guild of Editors, Fr. Slattery contributed immensely to labour and journalism.

Also during these years, he made remarkable contributions to the development of football and football administration in Nigeria. As an inside-left, he had played first division football in Lagos with the Lagos United. But it was as a referee that he made his greatest contribution. His Excellency, Nnamdi Azikiwe, first President of the Federal Republic of Nigeria, was Slattery's linesman in those days. He recalls that he made great strides as a referee probably because he was a Catholic priest; therefore, he was presumed honest. Rev. Fr. Denis Slattery was, at different times, the Chairman of the Referees' Association, Executive member of the Lagos Amateur Football Association, and Chairman of the Nigerian Football Association (N.F.A.)

In 1956, Archbishop Taylor invited Fr. Denis Slattery to establish a secondary school in Lagos. Fr. Slattery saw this assignment as an opportunity to contribute to society as an educationist and a sports administrator. Thus, in January, 1956, he founded St. Finbarr's College as a Technical Grammar School. Classes started on the premises of St. Paul's Primary School, Ebute Metta. St. Finbarr's College became the first school in Nigeria to run in duality a Technical and Grammar School. This was an innovation that endeared the school to parents. Fr. Slattery chose to name the school after Saint Finbarr, who was a great educator, a priest, and a bishop who founded a monastery of prayer and an institution.

In 1960, the school was approved by the Ministry of Education. By this singular action St. Finbarr's College became eligible to participate in the prestigious schoolboys' football competition, the Principal Cup. This had a special thrill for Rev. Fr. Slattery. He had one burning ambition since the day he founded St. Finbarr's College -- to win the prestigious Principal Cup! The name, St. Finbarr's College, was to become synonymous with schoolboy soccer and academic excellence in Nigeria.

Having moved from the premises of St. Paul's Primary School, Ebute Metta to its permanent site in Akoka in 1959, St. Finbarr's College made its debut in the Principal Cup in 1960. They lost to St. Gregory's College that year and in 1961. But in 1962, St. Finbarr's College won the Principal Cup. This was the beginning of unprecedented soccer supremacy in schoolboy football. The college went on to win the Principal Cup for a record nine times. The secret of this success was physical fitness, the provision of necessary training equipment, and a standard pitch (playing field). The myth goes to say that had Fr. Slattery coached the Nigerian national side of those days, they would have won the World Cup. Today, some of his concepts on football administration still remain valid.

Football was the delight of the students of St. Finbarr's; still, Fr. Slattery succeeded in pushing for excellence in other sporting endeavours. In 1960, the College made her debut in the Grier Cup. That year, Eddy Akika of St. Finbarr's College took the coveted Victor Ludorum Trophy winning the Hurdles, Long Jump, and second in the High Jump event.

Slattery ensured that sporting excellence was clearly tied to academic excellence. Through the years and on many occasions, the College had the enviable record of scoring a 100% pass in the WAEC entries. Thus, students of St. Finbarr's were noted for hard work and hard play. Today, Saint Finbarr's College has produced numerous Nigerians who got to the peak of their professional careers and contributed significantly to the development of the Nation. Notable amongst them are: Vice-Admiral Patrick Koshoni (Rtd.), Major-General Cyril Iweze, Nze Mark Odu, Otunba Anthony Olusegun Odugbesan, Dr. J. A. Ikem, Dr. Segun Ogundimu, Chief Empire Kanu P, Professor Steve Elesha, Dr. Tayo Shokunbi, Airvice Marshal Wilfred Ozah, Tom Borha, Segun Ajanlekoko.

Father Denis Slattery retired from St. Finbarr's College in 1975. He returned to his first love, his pastoral duties. So, to St. Denis Catholic Church, Bariga he retired; to a total service to the Church as Parish priest. He eventually retired as Vicar-General to the Archdiocese of Lagos, and left his footprints again, in the sand of time. Rev. Fr. Denis J. Slattery is a true Nigerian patriot of Irish parentage, who contributed to the pioneering of technical education in secondary schools and the growth of football administration in Nigeria. Rev. Fr. D. J. Slattery was a Missionary, Educationist, Journalist, Technocrat, Football Administrator, a mentor of sports, and one of nature's exceptional gentlemen.

Rev. Father Slattery was an outstanding example of the Irish Catholic Missionary movement, which in this century saw many thousands of Irish Reverend Fathers and Sisters leave Ireland to take the Christian message to the four corners of the world. He dedicated 56 years of his earthly life to the development of the Nigerian humanity. A keen sportsman and Journalist, he served

Nigeria in many capacities including Chairmanship of the Nigerian Football Association (NFA). He also edited the Catholic Herald Newspaper for many years. He brought with him from Ireland, a keen appreciation of the value of education, without which freedom, responsibility, or development is impossible. In his great desire to inform, Father Slattery became actively involved in the development of Journalism and Education. His major contribution to education, St. Finbarr's College, Akoka, is named after Saint Finbarr – the patron saint of his native county of Cork. His other enduring legacy to Nigeria, football, comes from his own passionate love of sport. Here, he obviously tapped into a rich vein in Nigerian life – a truly fanatical love of football. A list of his achievements and contributions is presented below.

Slattery's Achievements and Contributions

1. Vice-Chairman of the Society for the Bribe Scorners
2. Assistant Honorary Secretary of the Nigerian Olympic & British Empire Games Association
3. Publicity Secretary of the Lagos District Amateur Football Association
4. Member of the Council of African Students in North America
5. Assistant Secretary of the Nigerian Football Association
6. Honorary Secretary of the Commonwealth Games Appeal Fund
7. Catholic Representative of the Broadcasting Services (Religious)
8. Chairman of the Nigerian Referees Association
9. Chairman of the Council of Social Workers (Boy Scouts, Catholic Youth Organization, Salvation Army, Boys' Brigade, Y.M.C.A., Colony Welfare Organizations, Girls Guide, and Youth Clubs)
10. Chairman of the Leper Colony of Nigeria

11. Chairman of the Nigerian Football Association (NFA)
12. Editor of the Catholic Herald (Newspaper)
13. Foundation Member of the Nigerian Union of Journalists
14. Member of the Nigerian Guild of Editors
15. Founder and Principal of St. Finbarr's College, Akoka, Lagos
16. Founder of SS Peter & Paul, Shomolu
17. Founder of Our Lady of Fatima Private School, Bariga
18. Founder of St. Joseph's Vocational School, Akoka
19. Coordinator of the T.I.M.E. Project, Akoka
20. Founder of St. Finbarr's Catholic Church, Akoka, Lagos
21. Founder of St. Gabriel's Catholic Church
22. Founder of St. Flavius Catholic Church, Oworonshoki
23. Parish Priest of St. Denis Catholic Church
24. Vicar-General of the Catholic Church of Nigeria – Lagos Archdiocese (Rtd.)

Selected Quotes from Father Slattery's Book, *My Life Story*, West African Book Publishers, Limited, Ilupeju, Lagos, Nigeria, 1996.

Before his death, SFCOBA beseeched Father Slattery to give us his own account of the recollection of Saint Finbarr's College in the early days. Below what he told us:

"The Queen of England visited Nigeria during one of those years. When I bowed and shook hands with the Queen, I was quickly passed on to the Duke. The Queen took much more notice of the ladies in the line. Apparently, the Duke knew about my association with Football and refereeing. In the short conversation we had he made a very profound statement that I often used afterwards with an air of pride. The Duke of Edinburgh said to me, "Football is as good as its referee. A bad referee can spoil Soccer."

"But what has happened to our beloved country, one of the richest gems of Africa? What has become of all our dreams? How many have paid the supreme price sacrificing their lives at home and in foreign lands to build a new Nigeria? Literally thousands died in Egypt, North Africa, Burma, etc.

Look at Nigeria today, several years after independence. Today, sad to say, Nigeria is riddled with corruption from the top to the bottom. No segment of Nigerian Society is free from the Cankerworm of bribery that has eaten into the bowels of our nation."

"As a result of a lecture I gave one time when I blamed the budding political leaders that they had fallen very quickly for the flesh pots offered by the Colonialists by taking huge salaries as ministers with or without portfolios, (I stated that there was no Freedom in Nigeria but our neo-political leaders were dancing to the tune of the British overlords), the next day, I was on the receiving end of a few scathing remarks in the press.

One paper wrote, "Father Slattery must have been drugged or drunk. He could not see wood or the trees!!

But another paper replied, "Father Slattery is destined to be the 'Cardinal Minzenty' of Hungary to be sacrificed on the altar of British imperialism." I was neither. I was Catholic Priest that stood for freedom – freedom to worship the true God and to enjoy the good things of life."

"I always regarded the visit to the Holy Land as a gift from my people in Nigeria. Had I not come to Nigeria in the first place, I probably would not have ever visited those sacred places that are particularly dear to the Catholic Priest.

Thank you Nigeria for this wonderful gift on my 11th birthday, when I turned 44 years old. Don't forget that I am a Leap Year Child."

The Four Commandments of St. Finbarr's In Slattery's Time

Actually, there were "Four Commandments", not ten, strictly implemented to help maintain discipline. Any student violating these rules went down that "Corridor of no return." This had become a catch phrase in the school. These were the commandments:

Any student caught stealing will be expelled.

Any student caught copying at examination time will be expelled. Any student that fails is automatically expelled. He is not allowed to Repeat.

Any student leaving the compound during school hours without the Principal's permission will be expelled.

Any student caught smoking or with drugs will be expelled.

These were often discussed as the moral pillars of St. Finbarr's College, and the key to our policy. Proved beyond a shadow of doubt after thorough investigation, there was no mercy shown, even to a Form 1 Boy if caught breaking these decrees."

Everything about Father Slattery was for real and no lottery. He never sought fame and accolades. His approach was based on resolute pursuit rather than a game-of-chance undertaking. He pursued and did everything with resolute and unwavering commitment. He called each thing as he saw it. He was not a man of narrative pontification. He got to the point and that was it. Period.

To further appreciate my story, the reader must understand the background of Rev. Fr. Denis Slattery, the Irish priest who touched the lives of many Nigerians. He was an exceptional human being from the time he was born on 29th February, 1916 until his death on 10th July, 2003.

In a 1996 newspaper editorial, the writer Ochereome Nnanna presented an accurate characterization of Father Slattery on his eightieth birthday as a man of no flattery. A true renaissance man, Father Slattery said it as he saw it. All the accolades that Father Slattery has received over the years, both while he was alive and following his death, contain the same unmistakable fact. There was never any flattery about him. He was a man of no pretensions. What you saw was what you got from him. I have tried to pattern myself after him in that regard. A friend once called me "Deji of no pretensions." I still cherish that characterization.

Father Slattery prided himself as an Irish-Nigerian and has been credited with many contributions to the development of modern Nigeria (both pre-independence and following independence). He was a patriot to the core, an activist for righteousness not only from the standpoint of religion, but also from the points of social equality and political self-determination. His 1996 Memoirs, *My*

Life Story, published by West African Book Publishers, Ltd. gives a very detailed account of his contributions to Nigeria and Nigerians.

One admirable attribute of his work in Nigeria was his commitment to a non-parochial view of issues. He supported the views of different religious leanings, as long as the views matched the tenets of good citizenship. There was religious tolerance at St. Finbarr's College. There was tolerance of every economic status. Similarly, there was complete tribal and ethnic harmony at the school because Father Slattery saw to it that everyone accepted everyone else.

As Principal of Saint Finbarr's College from 1956 through 1975, Father Slattery used the threat of being expelled as a deterrent to discourage bad behavior by students. His common warning was "I will send you down that dirt road, and you will never come back, and God is my witness" He, of course, was referring to a one-way journey down the narrow dirt road of Akoka. Saint Finbarr's College campus was the one building in that area of Akoka at that time. It was a long dusty hike from the Unilag Road to the school with heavy bushes on either side of the road.

Father Slattery was a man of small stature. But his heart, energy, and enthusiasm matched those of a giant. He put his energetic temperament into good use in chasing misbehaving students around the school compound. With his robe flowing wildly in the wind, he would take off after boys that he suspected were contravening school rules. It was almost a game of cat and mouse. He monitored the school premises himself. Latecomers and those sneaking out of the school compound during the day hardly escaped his roving eyes. He could run. He could jump. He could even tackle ruffian boys and oh yes, he could really shout. He was a multi-faceted principal; and we all admired, revered, and feared him all at the same time. He also prided himself on being a boxer. Whether he was actually ever a boxer, or whether he put on that bluff to keep us in line, was a frequent debate among the students. When angered, he would challenge the students to a fistfight. Of course, he knew none of us would dare take him on, and he capitalized on that fact. Secondary school kids were much bigger in those days. We had classmates who were in their early twenties. Yet, none was big or man enough to confront the wrath of Father Slattery.

"Father is coming" was a frequent lookout call from boys doing what they were not supposed to be doing. Just like prairie dogs scenting an approaching predator, the boys would run helter-skelter in different directions. There would often be one unfortunate (slower) boy that would be chased down by Father. He would drag the boy into the principal's office for an appropriate punishment. At the next school assembly, we would all hear about the latest mischievous acts of "a few bad boys." I think Father Slattery probably enjoyed those encounters as a way to get his exercise in order to keep fit and trim. He was a nurturing disciplinarian. As strict as he was as a disciplinarian, Father Slattery was also a very forgiving individual. One minute he was shouting and ranting about something, the next minute he was patting you on the back for a good academic or football performance.

How he found the time, resolve, and energy to do all that he did was beyond explanation. Those of us who have tried to emulate his ways can usually be identified by our diverse interests both in avocation and recreation. Father Slattery was a very effervescent man; always excited and animated about everything. There was never a dull moment with him around.

6

How I got to Saint Finbarr's College

GETTING TO SAINT FINBARR'S College in 1968 paved the way for my eventual painting of the Rooster and the Hen in 1973.

In order to understand how Saint Finbarr's College transformed my life, one needs to know my own beginning and early years and how I came to cross paths with Rev. Fr. Slattery. I overcame several educational adversities before reaching my present educational attainment.

I was born on September 2nd, 1952, into the Sharafa Ola Badiru Onisarotu family of Epe, Lagos State. By the standard of the day, it was an affluent family. My father was a building contractor and traveled extensively in pursuit of his profession. Several of his children were, thus, born outside of Epe. He was a particularly popular person at Okegbogi Street in Ondo township in the late 1940s and early 1950s. I was only five years old when my father died prematurely on April 12, 1958. Thus, began the family hiatus that would disrupt what would have otherwise been a steady and sheltered upbringing. Because of his sudden death, his family was not prepared for how to manage and care for the younger children in the large family.

Fortunately, we had some grown children among us at that time. The adult children in the family "distributed" the younger ones among themselves to see to their upbringing. In the process, I was shuttled from one place to another, from one sibling to another, and from one extended relative to another. Over a period of a few years, I stayed with brothers, sisters, uncles, and some distant relatives. I had the good fortune of having a large and extended family with no shortage of good Samaritans willing to take me on as a ward.

The result of being a migrant ward was that I could not start school until 1961 — at the late age of nine! I started elementary school as Zumratul Islamiyyah Elementary school at No. 2, Tawaliu Bello Street, adjacent to Nnamdi Azikwe Road in the heart of Lagos in 1961. Thus, my first encounter with counting 1, 2, 3 and reciting A, B, C was not until I was nine years old. This late start, coupled with the fact that I started school in Lagos, where primary education was for eight years (in those days) compared to six years in the Western region, meant that I was five years behind my educational cohorts. But one thing that was in my favor at that time was my maturity level. At that age, I already understood the importance of education. I did not need any prodding or forcing to go to school. My level of maturity made me more attentive and appreciative of the teachers in the classroom, so; I was able to take in all lessons presented by the teachers. I did not need any supplementary lessons outside of school. In those days, teachers and observers erroneously attributed my better school performance (compared to my classmates) to my higher level of intelligence. For a long time, I mistakenly believed it too. But what was actually fueling the better academic performance was my higher maturity level. I enjoyed excellent rapport with my classmates and teachers. I could tell that the teachers not only liked me, but also respected me. For this reason, I never got into any punishment episode at school. I went through the entire elementary school without ever being flogged at school, in an age when school flogging was very rampant. The same record was later repeated throughout my secondary school years.

I suffered enough flogging at the homes of my guardians (for being rascally) to make up for the grace that I enjoyed at school. Contrary to the typical situation in those days, the school was my refuge. I enjoyed going to school in order to escape what I considered to be very oppressive disciplinary home environment. It happened that what, as a child, I considered to be oppressive chores at home turned out to be valuable lessons that still continue to serve me well at home until today. I still remain very handy at home, particularly in the kitchen and general household chores. My adoption of school as a refuge was fortuitous because it paved the way for my sound academic foundation. I knew I would not be able to study at home so I paid every bit of attention to the lectures at school. That way, I imbibed everything the teacher had to say. I never had an opportunity for supplementary lessons or studying at home. I relied entirely on school lectures. I could not afford not to pay attention at school. Children nowadays have the luxury of private lessons. Sometimes they get too lackadaisical about the opportunities.

In those days, I tended to have a freewheeling lifestyle of freedom to roam the neighborhood streets in search of play and fun. This did not sit well with my guardians, who preferred for me to be indoors to attend to household chores. So, I was frequently on a collision course with my guardians about my over-commitment to playing around the neighborhood. In spite of this rascally disposition, I still enjoyed good relationships with my guardians primarily because I still performed well in school. I recall an elderly neighbor intervening and pleading with one of my guardians to spare me a flogging on account of my school performance. He opined that, in spite of my playing too much, I was still doing very well at school compared to my playmates, who were playing and not doing well at school.

One of my favorite guardians was my uncle, the late Chief Alao Shabi. I learnt a lot of calm demeanor and rational mode of speaking from him. Although he flogged me a few times also, it was always at the instigation of unfair reports getting to him about what and what offense I had committed. Typical reports were about my being seen riding a bicycle around the neighborhood, swimming in a local public pool, or playing football on the playground. These were all considered dangerous and unauthorized acts in those days. That some of us learnt to ride bicycles, swim, and play football was a credit to our mischievous acts of running away from home for a few hours to engage in these fun but "dangerous" acts. My uncle was a scrap-metal dealer. He had a scrap-metal shop at Idumagbo in the heart of Lagos in the 1960s. His shop was later moved to Owode Onirin in the outskirts of Lagos. From 1965 through 1967, I helped him to tend the scrap metal shop along with his Hausa assistant, named Gaji. The general expectation was that after elementary school, I would become a full-time apprentice to my uncle and eventually go into the scrap metal business, which was a lucrative business in those days. My uncle engaged in exporting scrap metals overseas. So, he interacted with white expatriates through the ports at Apapa. The decades following Nigeria's independence saw a decline in the lucrative level of scrap metals. If I had gone into that business, I would probably be mired in the economic depression associated with it now.

I learnt a lot of hands-on activities from Gaji. He was the one who first introduced me to the properties of various metals and how to handle them. He gave me an early (albeit unscientific) appreciation for various metals. We sorted scrap metals into their respective categories. We dealt with mercury, silver, iron, steel, copper, brass, platinum, and other metals. I don't recall handling gold in those days. The hands-on skills still serve me well today in handling household tools. Even now, my most cherished possessions are the implements of household work such as hammers, pliers, screw drivers, drills, and so on. Anyone visiting my home now can hardly miss my intimate relationships with these implements.

I graduated from elementary school in 1967 and was to enter secondary school in January 1968. Because of my good academic performance and excellent result in the common entrance examination, it was generally believed that I would not encounter any difficulty in gaining admission into a secondary school. But there were other obstacles lurking beneath the raw academic record. What I thought should not matter in gaining admission into a reputable school (befitting of my common entrance results) were actually major obstacles in the eyes of the secondary school officials.

The prospects of not being able to pay school fees preempted my being admitted to the most reputable secondary schools. My sister, the late Mrs. Omowunmi Ayodele Durosimi (previously Mrs. Shojobi), insisted that I must go to a reputable high school because of her belief and confidence in my academic promise. She had monitored my performance throughout my elementary school and concluded that nothing but the best schools were appropriate for me. She, herself, had attended Queens School, Ede, in the Western Region. She had the vision of my attending such schools such as Kings College, Government College, and other well-known schools. Well, I applied to all those schools. Based on my common entrance examination results, I was invited for interview at all the schools. I was self-assured and confident about my academic-related performance at the interviews. But I was naïve about the other factors that were considered in admitting children to those schools. Frequently, at those interviews, I had no shoes on and wore the simplest of clothes. Being more mature than the other kids seeking admission, I always attended the interviews by myself. No accompanying parents, siblings, or relatives. If I had asked my family members, I could have received appropriate support to put on an "air" of being well-off enough to attend the schools. But I made a deliberate and conscious decision to attend the interview just as I was – without any pretensions. I was somehow arrogant about my academic capabilities, and I believed the school authorities would be impressed. But I was very wrong. My attitude going into the interviews was that I wanted to challenge the interviewers to ask me any question about school subjects so that I could impress them with my knowledge. But very often, questions were raised only about tangential elements that had nothing to do with school subjects. Some typical questions that I faced (and failed) were:

Who will pay your school fees?
Where is your father's house?
Did your mother attend a secondary school?
Has anybody in your family attended this school before?
Is your mother a trader or a government worker?
What is your professional goal?
Which elementary school did you attend?
Have you ever attended a nursery school?

The interviewers thought I would be a misfit at an Ivy-League type of secondary school. Although Zumratul Islamiyyah Elementary School was a good school on the inside, it was not highly regarded externally. This could be because it was located in the rough and tough inner-city part of Lagos Island. The street address of No. 2 Tawaliu Bello Street, adjacent to Nnamidi Azikwe Road, was noted more for commercial activities rather than as an academic base for a well-regarded school. The school had since been demolished and the site had been designated for other commercial purposes.

I had no doubt the other kids had been well-coached about the interview questions and had well-honed answers for all such silly questions. But I was brash and determined not to stoop too low as to give answers that would amount to pretensions. My sister had expected that many schools would be so impressed with my academic performance that they would admit me with scholarship offers. So, there was no prior arrangement or preparation by my family regarding how to pay my school fees. Frankly, my sister was caught off guard by the disappointing admission outcomes.

To be somewhat fair to the interviewers, my older age probably played against me. There I was trying to enter a secondary school at the ripe age of sixteen. I was five years older than my contemporaries seeking admission at the same time. Not knowing my history of starting school very late (at the age of 9), the interviewers very likely equated my advanced age to being slow in the elementary school. Their natural suspicion of my being academically dim did not match the documented performance on paper. So, they probably decided to err on the side of caution.

Zumratul did not have a secondary school at that time. Otherwise, I would have been a shoo-in to progress from Zumratul Elementary School to Zumratul Secondary School. So, I was like a goldfish out of a backyard pond looking to be placed in an ivy-league aquarium.

That I even attended Zumratul Elementary School had been by accident rather than by design. At my age of nine years in 1961, elementary schools were reluctant to enroll me. I was a raw and untested pupil with no prior preparation to enter school. The "raw" part of me at that time was what led to my moniker of "BB Raw-Raw" later on. BB stands for my middle and last names — Bodunde Badiru. I proudly autographed that insignia on my early drawings and paintings. The full salutation was "BB Raw-Raw, Broken Bottle Never Tires," whatever that was supposed to mean, I never knew. Many of my early friends still call me BB; but most people have forgotten or never knew of the Raw-Raw part of the motto.

In the search for my first elementary school, it happened that a sister-in-law, the late Mrs. Shadiyat Badiru, wife of my late brother, Mr. Atanda Badiru, was a book seller at the school at the time that an elementary school was being sought for me. She took me to the principal, who queried me about why I was just entering school for the first time. I was able to give him satisfactory answers because I was old enough to be cognizant of my situation and the consequences of my predicament. The principal was very impressed with my mature communication abilities. He decided to enroll me, jokingly making a comment that "Enu e dun," which satirically meant that my stories were tantalizing.

In 1967, I was invited to several Secondary School admission interviews. Notable among these were King's College, Lagos and Government College, Ibadan. None of these were successful. Even though the interview experiences were not successful, they were, nonetheless, very gratifying. The honor of being invited to interview at those schools brought much pride and joy to the officials of my elementary school. The interview at Government College, Ibadan, was a protracted one-week affair that culminated in written and oral tests on various subjects. I was informed that I did very well on the tests but did not meet the cut-off requirements in the overall interview. I returned to Lagos empty-handed.

After attending several interviews and not being successful, I concluded that I needed a better answer to the question of "Who will pay your school fees?" So, I embarked on an effort of seeking financial support from local philanthropists. One noted person that I appealed to was the late Chief S. B. Bakare. I had heard of several philanthropic projects that he had undertaken. I was hopeful that he would be so impressed by my academic potential that he might want to invest in my education. So, I crafted a well-written letter to him explaining my plight. The letter included carefully composed paragraphs that would indicate to him my knowledge and command of the English language, even at that age. I included statements about my common entrance exam results. I never received a response.

My disappointment was contained only by the prospects of contacting other philanthropists in Lagos. There was no shortage of such benefactors in Lagos in those days. Unfortunately, none of them came my way. All my attempts at pursuing philanthropic grace were futile. Years later, I began to understand why I might not have heard from those that I contacted. It could have been that they never received my letters at all because I did not have the correct addresses. It could also have been that their administrative assistants obstructed the delivery of the letters. Perhaps, they received thousands of requests, beyond what they could comfortably respond to or provide financial assistance for.

My admission to Saint Finbarr's College was nothing short of a miracle that manifested itself through the hands of Father Slattery. After several months on searching for a secondary school without success, the family's attention turned to exploring other options for my future. There were discussions of my going into some trade apprenticeship. A popular option was for me to capitalize on my drawing skills by going into a sign-writing business. Imagine the caption, "BB Raw-Raw Signs" or "BB, the Sign Writer" on a roadside kiosk.

That Saint Finbarr's College was considered as an option was due to a fortunate act of geographical proximity. I was living with my sister at the University of Lagos Staff Quarters at that time. She was then married to Dr. Wole Shojobi, who was then a Civil Engineering lecturer at the University. Having found no school yet, my sister decided that we should consider one of the local schools on the mainland of Lagos. Thus, Saint Finbarr's College came into the picture. Being in the immediate vicinity of Unilag, Finbarr's was a convenient choice.

The school was appealing because it was nearby and did not have a boarding school. Attending a boarding school far away would have compounded my financial inability to pay the school fees. My sister contacted Saint Finbarr's College and found out that there might be some openings in the school. It was already two weeks after school session started in January 1968. The fact that any openings existed at that time was a fortuitous coincidence. The school was looking for a few additional good students and I was looking for one good school. My sister sent me to the school to inquire. As usual, I went to the school all by myself.

It was a good thing that Reverend Father Slattery did not care what a prospective student looked like. I went to the school without shoes and no impressive "garmentry." Unlike my previous secondary school interview experiences, Father Slattery attended to me the same way he attended to all the parents who had come to the school with their kids to inquire about the "rumoured" openings. The Father was quite an impressive and blessed being. Although it was the first time that I would speak directly to a white man, I completely understood him and he understood me perfectly. I believe this is a credit to his years of living in Nigeria and communicating with various categories of Nigerians in local communities. He announced to everyone that there were **only three** vacancies. He cautioned that no parent should approach him to lobby for the open positions. He was going to fill the three vacancies purely on the basis of merit. There were several parents and kids in the audience when the announcement was made. I was the only unaccompanied boy in the group. By my own estimate, there must have been at least two hundred boys. I concluded that I had no chance, and presumed this to be another disappointing outcome in my lengthy and lonely search for a secondary school.

How was Father Slattery going to ensure a fair process of selecting only three kids from the hundreds that were interested in being admitted? He laughed at the parents' inquiry. He responded that he had an ingenious plan. He told everyone to come back on some specified date. He did not say what the selection plan was. I believe he kept the plan secret to preempt any attempt by any parent to usurp the process. Without knowing the selection process, no one knew how to prepare or scheme for success. He told everyone there was no need for the kids to prepare anything for the appointed date. Just show up on time. Disappointed, everyone left for that day. I was filled with misgivings about the whole thing. But I was heartened by the fact that I was still in the running.

On the appointed day, I showed up at the school, unaccompanied, as usual. Father Slattery told everyone to assemble in the open field across from the Assembly Hall. There were hundreds of anxious eyes. There were murmurings among the parents regarding what was going on; and what was going to happen. Father Slattery stepped onto the high concrete pavement bordering the Assembly Hall. This position gave him an elevated view of the audience. It was like being on a high-rise podium. After positioning himself majestically in front of and above the audience, he announced that he was going to select three kids from the audience to fill the open vacancies on the basis of the common entrance exam results. Everyone was baffled. How was he going to do that? Father asked two clerks from the school office to come onto the pavement. A table and a chair were hurriedly positioned on the pavement. The clerks had been inside the Assembly Hall (as if on a secret mission), waiting for Father's instruction to emerge. After the clerks were appropriately settled, with one sitting on the chair and the other standing beside the table with papers and pencils in hand, Father Slattery beckoned to the school secretary, I believe her name was Monica, to bring out a big pile of typed sheets, the like of which I had never seen until then. The pile must have measured almost one foot above the table. People in the audience looked at one another anxiously. No one knew what was about to unfold.

As I would become aware later on during my days at Saint Finbarr's, Father Slattery's antics at getting things done often bordered on craziness. He was a renegade of a person. He had a penchant for the unexpected. His ways of doing things were replete with surprises, wonderment, curiosity, and suspense. He could have been a successful movie star.

Father Slattery was a man of small stature, but with a giant personality. Although his height was reported as just over five feet, he had a huge reach that could intimidate any large person. He claimed to have been a kid boxer in his hometown of Fermoy, Ireland. Watching his temper and impatience with unruly boys, no one dared doubt his claim to the pugilistic record of his youth. He was reported as having the physical ability to jump up to slap an erring school boy to bring him back down to Earth in behavior. Although I never witnessed such an occasion myself, I did believe it.

Father Slattery would always find unusual and amusing ways to get things done. I think that was by a deliberate design by him. Through his unconventional approach, he got a lot of attention. Once he got your attention, he could then impose his will on you. People were often amused, rather than being offended, by his unusual and eccentric ways. He had a volatile temperament to match his odd ways. But no one dared challenge him. So, everyone waited patiently for him to announce his grand plan. He hesitated in announcing his plan deliberately to keep the audience in suspense and partly to disarm any rancor from the audience. Father Slattery often operated like a shrewd psychologist. He had all kinds of ingenious means of dealing with people. That was why he was so beloved throughout Nigeria. I don't think he ever lost an argument in his heydays. When discussions didn't go his way, he would put on a fake tantrum in order to still get his way. People usually succumbed to him by simply laughing in amazement of his antics. He was an all-encompassing person: a Revered Clergyman, a comic (if need be), a humorist (if necessary to lighten the moment), a runner (chasing after mischievous kids), a boxer (if needed to mete out a punishment), and a sportsman to the core. Except for his clergy robes, his restless ways revealed no sign that he was a Catholic priest. It was not until his later years, in a slowed state of physical being, that anyone could rein him in.

Well, with all the suspense over, Father Slattery announced that the clerks would start reading names off the pile of common entrance examination results. The pile of computer paper contained the list of common entrance results in merit order. Names would be read from the list until the three highest scoring boys in the audience were identified. This process was baffling because there was no way to ensure when the three names would be found among those kids in the audience. Father maintained that if all the kids in the audience had taken the common entrance examination in Lagos State, then their names would appear somewhere in the list of results, even if they were at the far end of the list. Father Slattery said he was prepared to continue this exercise until the highest three had been identified, even if it took days. Being enmeshed in the crowd, I could hear hisses from some parents. Were they prepared to commit that kind of indefinite time, with no assurance of success in the end? Some parents tried to get Father's attention for private discussions. But he refused. Even the highly-placed, obviously rich, and well-connected parents in the audience could not sway Father Slattery from his determined approach. Many parents tensely tried to explain the process to their kids. Being alone, I had no one to explain anything to me. Instead, I eavesdropped on the covert mumblings deep within the recesses of the crowd.

Unconcerned, Father Slattery motioned to the clerks to start reading out the names. So it was that we embarked on this journey of the seemingly endless reading of names. I started praying fervently inwardly to be one of the three selected. Being of small stature, and having only myself to account for, I gradually pushed my way to the front of the crowd. I positioned myself right in front of the clerks' table. I was occasionally pushed back by one of the clerks, wanting to create sufficient elbow room for the prevailing task. At one time, Father Slattery threatened to end the process if the audience crowded the clerks too closely. But realizing the anxiety among the audience, he relented. So, my position was secured very close to the face of the person reading the names.

Names were read on and on. The process went on for several hours without anyone acknowledging the names read so far. Being at the edge of the table, I could scan each page of the list as soon as the clerk opened it, before the reading of that page started. When my name was not on the list, I would pray silently so that no one else in the audience would be on that page. The process had started around 9a.m. It must have been around 1p.m. when the first name from the audience was found. The first successful name found was Francis Egbuniwe.

So, one position out of three was gone. I had only two more chances of entering Saint Finbarr's College. I intensified my silent prayers. But instead of being picked second, someone else was picked to fill the next open position. The second successful name found was Joseph Molokwu.

After what seemed like more endless hours, I spotted my name about the middle of a newly opened page. I screamed, "That's my name, that's my name, on this page, that's my name." "My name is here!," sticking my finger at my name listed on the page. This unauthorized announcement caught everyone off guard. I was shouted at to keep quiet. Names must be read from the top to the bottom. There would be no interjection to the middle of the page. When the clerk got to that point, the name would be called. So, I kept quiet as chided. I further intensified my silent prayers. "God, let no one else be called ahead of my name on that page." I am sure that the Good Lord was listening to my juvenile prayers. The third, and final successful name found was Bodunde Badiru.

Although the passage of time has eroded my recollection of the exact events of that day, the agony of the tense waiting has remained etched in my memory. In later years at the school, Francis, Joseph, and I, along with Joseph's close friend, Michael Elumeze, would engage in endless debates as to who was picked first, second, or third. I still feel the torment of waiting to be picked third. So, I remember the order clearly. Father Slattery came back onto the scene to formalize the selection of the three kids. He announced that these three kids were the new students of Saint Finbarr's College.

1. Francis Egbuniwe (now late)
2. Joseph Molokwu
3. Bodunde Badiru

They must show up to start classes in the morning, without delay. School had already started two weeks earlier. So, we must start attending classes forthwith.

Thus, I began my secondary school education at Saint Finbarr's College in January 1968. Father Slattery handled the admission process his own way. It was fair, just, and transparent. It was right there in the open field. No flattery, no pretensions. There were no private meetings. There were no under-the-table deals. It was the only way I could have entered a reputable secondary school in 1968. All other doors had been slammed shut. Father Slattery opened the door of educational opportunity for me, without consideration of age, color, creed, race, tribe, language, financial status, political leaning, or religious affiliation. It was totally on the basis of merit. He let the best in the pool of prospective students rise to the top to claim the three prized positions. Can you see my point now? It was a special blessing for me. I hope readers can now understand why writing this book (the third in a series) is very special for me. I cannot imagine going to my grave without committing this story to a published book. I am extraordinarily indebted to Father Slattery. Writing this book is the only way I can reward his kindness and fairness. Leaders of today and tomorrow should learn a lot from Father Slattery's ways.

My life has been intimately intertwined with events associated with Saint Finbarr's College. My life then and my life now still bear remarkable allegiance to some memorable events during my days at the school. I had many good times at Saint Finbarr's College. My classmates from those Finbarr's days are still my buddies today, to whatever extent we can still stay connected and in touch. The fun of my Class IIIA and the faces in our class photo remain etched in my memory.

Mr. Kpotie, who later became a Finbarr's principal, was our biology teacher in that class year. I often served as the illustrator for the Biology class. As the teacher wrote notes on the board, I did the biology drawings to accompany the notes. Because my Biology, Chemistry, and Physics notes were always complete and well-illustrated, many times, my classmates borrowed my notebooks to make up their own notes at home. Using my artistic interest, I hand-embossed Saint Finbarr's logo on the cover of each notebook.

So much did I adore my biology, chemistry, and physics lessons that I later coined the following quote on the subjects, with respect to my 2010 book on **"The Physics of Soccer: Using Math and Science to Improve Your Game."**

> *"Biology determines what we are, Chemistry explains what makes us what we are, and Physics describes what we do."* - Deji Badiru

I was particularly close to all my classmates, but those that I ran around town with most often were Joseph Molokwe, Michael Elumeze, and Abimbola Aibinu. My relationships cut across all genres of classmates. Other close classroom associates were Babatunde Ogunde, Olawale Adewoyin, Philip Bieni, Charles Azoume, and the late Francis Egbuniwe.

My passion for reading and writing extensively originated from my days at Saint Finbarr's College. My series of books on the Physics of Soccer (2010, 2014, and 2018) were inspired by the sports legacy acquired at Saint Finbarr's College. My Finbarr's ID card and my Ebute-Metta neighborhood soccer club ID card are two of my cherished items from those days. The Finbarr's ID card was signed personally by Father Slattery himself, as he did for all students at that time.

In my Finbarr's days, I read voraciously by checking out books from the Yaba Public Library. I, especially, loved the American Cowboy Western Novels for their exceptionally expressive description of the rugged terrains and the tough cowboys.

I have remained in true and in frequent touch with Saint Finbarr's College. During my induction into the Nigerian Academy of Engineers (NAE) in 2006, a team of SFC students attended and participated in the great accomplishment. I was as proud of the students' SFC vests as they were of my NAE induction regalia. As an ex-Finbarrian, I continue to participate in promoting SFC at home and abroad in consonant with fellow ex-Finbarrians.

Starting at Saint Finbarr's College was not easy at first. Since I had to start classes the very next day after I was miraculously admitted, I was totally unprepared. I had no uniform, still no school shoes, and no books. My sister, the late Mrs. Durosimi (Mrs. Shojobi at that time) had generously agreed to pay my school fees. But the arrangement was for my mother to pay for my books, uniforms, and other essential items. Therein lay the initial obstacles. My mother was not immediately prepared for such responsibilities. She was a petty trader, plying her migrant trade between Ondo Township, Atijere, Okitipupa, Ejinrin, and Epe. She was so overjoyed that I had gained admission into a secondary school that she pledged to sell her prized jewelries and family heirlooms to raise the money needed to carry out her own end of the bargain. But, selling those things required some time. So, there was a time lag between when I had to start classes and when my mother could buy my uniforms, shoes, and books.

Father Slattery allowed me to attend classes for one whole week without uniform before sending me home. This was an unmistakable message that I needed to get my school uniform by hook or crook. Somehow my mother was able to come up with the money for my uniform. As for the books, Father Slattery allowed me to borrow some books from the school library. Gradually, I settled into the business of my secondary school education.

Although Father Slattery knew me personally at that time because of the way I entered the school, but what really brought us close together was a miscue that I committed in his religious studies class. In one of the early examination questions that I faced in his class, I missed the definition of immaculate conception. What I presented as the definition was the exact opposite of the answer. The error must have been due to my lack of knowledge or a temporary gap in my train of thought. I can't quite explain how the error occurred. But the result was that Father Slattery was very furious. His brow wrinkled up. He curled his lips as if searching for the right words to blurt out. Finally, he confided that I had committed blasphemy. "Son, you have sinned. The thing you should have done was to not write anything if you knew you did not know the answer," he exclaimed. "I will have to pray for you." I believed he made such a big deal of the issue not just because of the error itself, but because he wanted to make sure that I got the message. And yes, indeed, I got the message, and I have never forgotten it. That incident encouraged me to never let any point of religious studies slide through my fingers again. Thereafter, I became one of the best students in Father Slattery's classes. This is an example of how Father Slattery used shrewd antics to get the attention of students. It was a clever mind game that he played to get students to perform at their best.

Discipline was and still is a major attribute and attraction of Saint Finbarr's College. Parents take delight in the discipline that kids get at the school. The mantra of the school revolve around three tenets of:

1. Academics
2. Football
3. Discipline

The school was widely noted for these. Father Slattery provided the educational infrastructure to pursue academics. He also provided the sports environment to ensure the accomplishment of an esteemed football prowess. Finally, he conjured the physical presence to impose discipline on everyone. There was a rule for everything. Abiding by those rules helped in shaping the future outlook of the students.

Cartoon experiments in the art room of Saint Finbarr's led to a brief opportunity to draw cartoon strips for the children's page of the Daily Times of Nigeria newspaper in 1970 and 1971. My cartoon column was dubbed **"Fun with BB."** The art teacher and Father Slattery were very proud of this "educational outreach" as they called it because I had a contract and got paid for the cartoons that were published in the newspaper. This was a big accomplishment for a high school kid in those days. Father Slattery was particularly impressed because the school was still relatively young and needed to build a good reputation in other areas apart from football. So, he would widely commend and publicize any outside accomplishments of students of the school.

Hm-m-- Mummy is not so careless with her money.

While I was at Saint Finbarr's, I played on the mosquito and rabbit football teams. These were the junior level teams designed to prepare boys for the full-fledged first-eleven team later on. My self-proclaimed nickname for playing football was "Iron Pillar." Some of my fun-loving classmates (notably Benedict Ikwenobe) translated the nickname into different variations. These invoked a lot of fun and laughter whenever we were on a playing field. Although I was a decent player, I was never committed to being on the regular team of Saint Finbarr's College. Late Mr. Anthony Onoera (former principal), while coaching our rabbit team, lamented that if I would fully commit to playing football, I could be a superb Finbarr's player. Of course, the competition for securing a spot on the regular team was incredibly keen and I wasn't fully committed to training to be a regular soccer player. Saint Finbarr's College football players were of a different stock – highly skilled and talented. Many of them, even in high school, could have played on professional teams. In fact, the 1970 team was so good that there was a plan to have the team play the professional team Stationery Stores. But the untimely death of Chief Israel Adebajo, the owner of Stationery Stores, just one day before the scheduled match, scuttled the plan. So, we never got to find out if our high school team could have beaten a full-fledged professional team. In my later years, recalling my Saint Finbarr's soccer heritage, I did blossom into a more respectable recreational player. I played on my university team in Tennessee and later on adult recreational teams in Florida and Oklahoma.

Inter-house sports were another big part of the experience at Saint Finbarr's College. Although I participated in several sports at the school, I was always only on the fringes of excellence in each one. My primary goal was more to be a part of the fun of sports. I don't recall devoting the necessary training time needed to excel. But I occasionally used the pretext of going for sports training at the school to escape from home so that I could go and play elsewhere. My sister always gave me permission to go out if I connected the reason to some sports activity at the school. She knew sports was very important at Saint Finbarr's and she never wanted to interfere with the school's expectations.

Following my enrollment at Saint Finbarr's College, I occasionally stayed with my sister at the Unilag Staff Quarters. Whenever she did not have a house help, I would move in with her to provide household support covering all manners of household chores including kitchen service and gardening. My present affinity for the kitchen and household chores was shaped in those years. Living so close to the college often created temptations for us to sneak out of school during school hours. This was a no-no according to the rules of the school. But young boys always enjoy the challenge (and perils) of doing what they are told not to do. If we managed to sneak out without being caught by Father Slattery, we would visit the homes of classmates living at Akoka and make the long trek to Lagoon at the edge of Unilag campus – in search of fun and play. Thinking back now, it was a big risk. I can never explain why we would have risked being permanently expelled from the school. Whenever we successfully got out and back to the school compound, we would feel a sense of great accomplishment. With that euphoria, we would start looking forward to the next opportunity to sneak out again. I thank God that no one in my group of friends was ever caught engaging in this mischievous act. Boys that were caught faced the full wrath of Father Slattery. I did my best to stay out of such wrath. In fact, I earned a good Testimonial from Father Slattery when I graduated. He was never bashful to write straight testimonials, whether good or bad. He signed every document directly by himself. Original documents signed by Father Slattery are highly-priced documents by those who had the good fortune to have received a signed document from him.

A December 1998 Christmas Card from Father Slattery to the Badiru Family contains his usual statements of blessings. The card remains a cherished item in the family's collection of memorable items. The greetings, in Father Slattery's own aged handwriting, reads as follows:

"Dear Adedeji B. Badiru

Congratulations for all the letters from U.S. and also thank you for the Video. Received it here in Ireland on Twenty-third November 1998.

I hope a member of my family will tape it and send a copy to our Boss – Blackock Road, Cork. It will be kept in the Archives and probably used occasionally to help the cause of the Mission.

I was very proud of all the old boys who appeared on the Video. Your speeches were wonderful. You made it a historic and unique occasion.

You will be happy to know that I am all set for my return journey to Lagos –

I hope to continue for some time the work of the Mission and pay a special attention to Finbarr's and the old boys and the new.

Thanks for all you have done for the Alma Mater.

Greet your wife and children. May God Bless you all.
Happy and holy Christmas.
God bless you.
Denis Slattery"

It is a fact that Saint Finbarr's College adequately prepared me for the challenges, tribulations, and triumphs of life; following my completion of my secondary school education. This is the same story that every graduate of the school proudly proclaims. Around town, Finbarr's boys enjoyed special privileges, which many were quick to flaunt. "Omo Father Slattery" (Father Slattery's kid) was a common moniker for Finbarr's boy around Lagos in those days.

By the time I left Saint Finbarr's College in December 1972, my fun days of Lagos were slowing ebbing. 1970 represented the height of my enjoyment of Lagos streets. Starting in 1973, several other things were beginning to creep into my life. I still wanted to continue my association with my neighbourhood friends. I belonged to informal clubs dedicated to having fun in the neighbourhoods. There was the Lagos Island Rascals and there was The Kano Street Gang at Ebute Metta. In 1966, I had lived with my uncle at Bamgbose Street right across from Campus Square. I made several friends on the tough playgrounds of campus square. In my various living arrangements with relatives between 1961 and 1972, I had resided at various locations in the Lagos Metropolis. I had lived at Andrew Street, Lagos; Tokunboh Street, Lagos; Bamgbose Street, Lagos; Ita Alagba Street, Lagos; Kano Street, Ebute Metta; Brickfield Road, Ebute Metta; Bode Thomas Street, Surulere; and University of Lagos Staff Quarters.

Even after finishing secondary school, I still enjoyed cruising many of the fun neighbourhoods of my previous habitats. My family started to worry about my future. They were concerned that I was nonchalant and indifferent about my future. They deplored my interest in attending parties in Lagos. They wanted me to aggressively start seeking admission to a university. But I would always defend myself by claiming that I knew "what I was doing." I maintained that I had everything under control. Underneath the party image, I had a structured and determined mind focused on being successful with whatever I wanted to do. Father Slattery had imparted the discipline of success in all his students; and I was sure I was not going to end up destitute. My attitude was "Let me enjoy myself for now; success is destined to come later on."

That I met and married my wife was due to an act of coincidence that had its roots in the Art Room of Saint Finbarr's College. Had I not attended Saint Finbarr's College; had I not been in the school's art room painting a colorful rooster; had I not been in good favour with the art teacher; had the art teacher not given me a job referral to Mr. Nupo Samuel at the Lagos State Ministry of Education – Audio Visual Aids Section; had I not returned to the painting of the colorful rooster; I would not have my wife of today. It was a step-wise progression from Saint Finbarr's College art room to the eventual liaison with my future wife. The painting that started at Saint Finbarr's College art room culminated in the rooster and the hen characters in this book. To this date, that 1973 painting has remained a favorite feature of our home decoration.

Meeting Iswat was what purged me of the Lagos street demons that were plaguing me. If I had not met her at that time, my care-free, fun-loving, and reckless partying around Lagos could have derailed my professional future. I was a good dancer with incredible staying stamina on the dance floor. So, I was frequently sought after at Lagos party events as a "life of the party." You might say I was footloose and fancy free. That reputation was what led to the objection of Iswat's sister, Mrs. R. Omosanya, popularly called Alhaja, when she found out that I was dating her sister. She cautioned, "That boy has a popular reputation among the Broad Street and Ministry girls. You should stay away from him. He would use you and dump you." This was an erroneous and undeserved reputation. I was popular for my party dancing, but I actually did not have many girlfriends. In fact, I had no girl friend at all when I met Iswat. I was spending so much time on the dance floors that I did not devote sufficient time to wooing a girl. Seeing how girls were anxious to dance with me at parties, some people concluded erroneously that I must be dating several girls. I wish I was; but that was not the case.

On the dance floor, I was transformed into a different person, possessed by the rhythms of good music, any type of music at all. I rarely ate or drank at parties. My entire focus was always on my dance steps. I was always a spectacle to watch at Lagos parties of those days.

My interest in permanently preserving my dancing repertoire led to my creating my "Dancing Professor" videotape later on in the USA. That video never saw any level of distribution because my wife found it embarrassing and thought it did not befit my other reputation as a learned professional. I still covertly keep a few copies of the videotape, and I sneak them out of the house every now and then to show to my friends, if they promise not to tell my wife that they have seen the tape.

I thank Saint Finbarr's College for creating the pathway to meeting my beautiful and faithful wife. It was through Saint Finbarr's College that I met my art teacher. It was through the art teacher that I met Mr. Nupo Samuel. It was through Mr. Samuel that I ended up at the Audio-Visual Aids Section of the Lagos State Ministry of Education. It was through that work place that Iswat walked into my life. It was the painting exercise that started at Saint Finbarr's Art Room that finally softened Iswat's heart towards me. If not for Saint Finbarr's College, I would not have met her, at least not in the context that eventually united us as husband and wife.

7

Continuation of the Blessings

THE BLESSINGS OF SAINT Finbarr's College continued to follow me into the years beyond high school. While I was still working at Lagos State Ministry of Education, I came across an advertisement for clerks at Central Bank of Nigeria (CBN). I applied and was fortunate to secure employment as Clerk Grade C. I was posted to the Staff Pay Office. I joined CBN in April 1974. Iswat was still working at the ministry. But CBN was a short trekking distance from the ministry. So, we did not feel physically disconnected. It was at Central Ban that I met Mr. Supo Adedeji (now late), who later became a close friend and a selfless helper in my pursuits of overseas scholarships later on. I was not thinking of an immediate departure for overseas studies because I had Iswat to think of.

Central Bank was conducting a certificate review of all staff sometime late in 1974. That was when several senior administrators came in contact with my school cert results. I was summoned to the office of Alhaji Elias, who was then a department head. He chastised me for not putting my high school performance to good use. He felt such a school cert result should be leveraged to pursue further studies overseas. I told him I was planning to go abroad for further studies, but I had not saved enough money yet. My family members were already concerned that I was whiling away my post-secondary schools. It was suspected that I was getting carried away with the fun life of Lagos and was not interested in furthering my education. Alhaji Elias' concern only served to confirm the fears of my family. He insisted that I must apply for scholarships to facilitate my further studies forthwith. When I subsequently secured Federal Government scholarships, he willingly served as one of my guarantors. Other individuals serving as my guarantors for the scholarship offers were Mr. Nupo Samuel and my brother, the Late Mr. Atanda Badiru. Father Slattery continued to provide written testimonials as required for many of my scholarship and university admission processes. Such was his dedication to the welfare and success of his students that he always found the time to provide written recommendations.

In December 1975, I proceeded to the USA to start my studies in Industrial Engineering at Tennessee Technological University. I was on a full scholarship from the Federal Government of Nigeria. Iswat came to join me in the USA in June 1976. So began my academic and professional pursuits in the USA. The sojourn started with a grand sendoff party by my Central Bank buddies. In the USA, I reconnected with the late Mr. Francis Osili, a close friend in my Central Bank office. He went to study in Wisconsin while I went to study in Tennessee. We had many years of social exchanges until his passing in 2017. May his generous soul rest in peace.

In the summer 1984, I visited Nigeria for the first time in eight years.; my first visit home after going to the USA in December1975. It was during that visit that my sister reunited me with Father Slattery. She was very proud of my academic achievement in the USA and wanted Father Slattery to be aware of what I had accomplished so far. We visited Father Slattery at his Akoka home. He had been displaced as the principal of the Saint Finbarr's College by that time. It was a very sad feeling for me to see him not on the school compound, but in a secluded house. No longer was he engaged in doing what he loved most – running Saint Finbarr's College. He recounted how bored he was for not being involved in school affairs. But at the same time, he was grateful that he then had time to devote more energy to the Church.

During the visit, Father Slattery instructed me to consolidate whatever I was planning to do on behalf of SFCOBA with what Segun was already doing. He was full of praise for Segun and his exceptional leadership skills. Since that time, Segun and I have worked closely with other dedicated Finbarrians to advance the cause of SFCOBA and the school.

I entered the academic career primarily because of my interest in following the educational lineage established by Reverend Father Slattery.

Later on, as Dean of University College at the University of Oklahoma, I tried my best to help students, foreigners and Americans alike, with their educational objectives. This created an immense gratification for me. One enters the teaching profession, not because of the financial rewards possible, but because of the opportunity to impart knowledge to others. "Teach onto others as you have been taught" is my premise for teaching. I have continued this same philosophy in all my professional pursuits.

Recalling the discipline impacted by my years at Saint Finbarr's College, I created what I called the equation of success for my students. The axiom, referred to as "Badiru's Equations of Success," entreats students to rely more on their self-discipline in accomplishing goals and objectives. The equation says that success is a function of three primary factors: raw intelligence, common sense, and self-discipline.

$$S = f(x, y, z),$$

Where:
x = Intelligence, which is an innate attribute, which every one of us is endowed with.

y = Common sense, which is an acquired trait from our everyday social interactions.

z = Self-Discipline, which is an inner drive (personal control), which helps an individual to blend common sense with intelligence in order to achieve success.

With this equation, success is within everyone's control. One cannot succeed on intelligence alone. Common sense and self-discipline must be used to facilitate success.

On October 1, 1998, several Old Boys and I were inducted into the esteemed order of "Distinguished Conqueror (DC)" of Saint Finbarr's College, an exalted position of recognition for Finbarr's Alumni. Friends and family members accompanied me to the event at Sheraton Hotel. The installation accompanied the establishment of the annual distinguished lecture series, which took place on October 7, 1998. Prof. Awele Maduemezia was the main inaugural speaker. Father Slattery's speech delivered at the inaugural lecture typified his life-long service to Nigeria. He was in Ireland at the time and could not attend to deliver the speech in person. But the power of the words contained in the prepared speech represented him so very well, as if he was there in person.

"Welcome to all – distinguished lecturer, parents, audience and students.

Many months ago, the President of St. Finbarr's, Segun Ajanlekoko, told me that the Executive Committee of the Finbarr's Old Boys were planning on inaugurating an annual distinguished guest lecture. To be truthful, I pooh-poohed the whole idea. I asked myself how a comparatively young College could launch such an august event in a city like Lagos, where there are many educational colleges and universities of great distinction.

Is St. Finbarr's going to be the first college to honor their first Principal? Why?

The more I thought about it, the more I realized that the proposed lecturer of today has launched, I am sure, many First Lectures before now. But it occurs to me that it is the first time that a secondary school Principal was to be honored by past pupils in this way.

Today's Guest Speaker is Professor Awele Maduemezia, the former Vice-Chancellor of Edo State University, Ekpoma. Our speaker today is the first Nigerian to gain a Ph.D. in Physics. Another Professor – an Old Boy – will be honored with A.D.C. (Distinguished Conqueror Award).

This will be the first time that your first Principal does not know personally the distinguished lecturer. You are welcome, Sir.

The topic is "Education, Yesterday Years, Today, and Tomorrow."

I do not want to pre-empt one iota what the lecturer will say in his lecture, but I will still say that the vast majority of those educated "Yesterday Years" were educated on a par with the present school system.

Long before I came to Nigeria in 1941, there was a Rev. Father Stephen Woodley, SMA, born in 1887 at Chester in the Diocese of Shrewsbury, England. He came at a time when nearly all the priests were continentals. The colonial Government launched great pressure on the missionaries to supply English-speaking priests and Reverend Sisters, capable of running good schools. Fr. Stephen Woodley was there-and-then appointed in charge of the Catholic schools in Lagos and environs. The imbalance in the number of Catholic schools and the Government schools soon became very apparent. There were 34 schools with nearly 4000 pupils only. Eleven of these schools were under the colonial Government.

The Head Masters and the teachers were certified native teachers, but in the Girls' schools, each student was taught by a European Sister.

In the Grammar School (at Holy Cross), Rev. Fr. Herber, SMA, taught Latin and French languages and the Principal, Fr. Woodley himself, took higher classes in the different English branches.

Herewith, a sentence recorded in the Archives: `The Catholic Schools in Lagos can compare favorably with the best schools in the country and our boys are admired by all ... for their spirit of obedience and discipline.

The above were the children of Yesterday. What of the children of Today? They were more fortunate. Our children of Today received a more thorough education parallel with the English school system.

The archives tell us that Father Woodley held that post up to 1927 and enjoyed good health. He set a glorious example by building new schools and colleges, taking an interest also in games, especially in soccer. Unfortunately, in that year 1927, he was injured in the back and had to return to England.

At that time, both the policy of the Church and the colonials realized that education must be urgently pursued. Many young Catholic priests gave their lives, stricken down by Yellow Fever, Black Water Fever, and Malaria, having lived only for a few years in tropical Nigeria.

Yet, it could be said that the pupils of Today (1930-1960), both at the primary school level, the secondary school and teacher training levels rivaled the colonial efforts to give a decent education to the rising generation at that time. Our products of Today became the basic rock of future education as we sailed into the education of "Tomorrow."

At this stage – the year of Independence 1960 – Nigerians took charge of their own country and initiated a new and most daring education policy. The third education Tomorrow had arrived.

There is no need to deny the fact that here in Nigeria, we followed step-by-step, the British Education Policy, punctuated with ultra-modern ideas borrowed from America and Europe. No longer did the new Ministry of Education confine our children to nine subjects. Even at the primary level, there were splits and choices up to twenty subjects. Every big subject was shrunk and all were added to the School Certificate Examination for the secondary schools; for boys and girls.

All of us now know that there are very obvious weaknesses in Tomorrow's education system, but let us leave that to our distinguished Physics lecturer. Please enlighten us all on Education Yesterday Years, Today, and Tomorrow.

We anticipate you will write your own name in the pages of history by an honest analysis of nearly 140 years of education. Undoubtedly, you will lift the veil that has clouded our thinking in the past and brighten the future of the present student body.

We hope that their future will be brighter and also the future of the parents who are dedicated to give the best to their children.

We pray that those in administration will be honest and not afraid to purge the canker worms that have eaten into our present efforts. After all, education is the light of the world. May it shine on all of us.

The activities of the Saint Finbarr's College Old Boys Association North America (SFCOBA – North America) moved forward rapidly in 2001, mainly due to the reconnection efforts of Dr. John Nwofia. While I was seeking out old Boys from across the USA and Canada, Dr. Nwofia was doing exactly this same thing out of his professional base in Nashville, Tennessee. It was in this concurrently effort that he contacted me via email in 2001 and inquired if I was interested in linking up with former students of Saint Finbarr's College. I excited responded affirmatively. We subsequently arranged reciprocal meetings at my home in Knoxville, Tennessee and his home in Nashville, Tennessee. Mr. Kenny Kuku and Mr. Olawale Adewoyin also attended those meetings and we scheduled additional meetings at Kenny's home in Atlanta and Olawale's home also in Atlanta.

Frequent discussions and reconnections with additional ex-Finbarrians led to the emergence of our annual SFCOBA – America annual reunions. Annual reunions have since taken place as listed below:

Reunion 2012: Atlanta, Georgia, USA
Reunion 2013 (West Palm Beach, Florida)
Reunion 2014 (Nashville, Tennessee)
Reunion 2015 (Baltimore, Maryland)
Reunion 2016 (Houston, Texas)
Reunion 2017 (Chicago, Illinois)
Reunion 2018 (Atlanta, Georgia)

At the 2013 Reunion, I was presented with the DJ Slattery Excellence Award by the SFCOBA North America. For this recognition, I was (and still remain) very grateful.

It was all fun, games, and reminiscing chatter at the Inaugural Annual Reunion of SFCOBA-North America in Atlanta, Georgia on September 1, 2012. A formal meeting was held to kick off the reunion. There was a specially-crafted celebratory cake for the occasion. After nine months of preparation, the reunion went on without a hitch. **Otunba Anthony Awofeso** and **Professor Adedeji Bodunde Badiru** headed the chronology of the Boys in attendance with their Class of 1972 lapel pins. Great thanks and appreciation go to Kenny Kuku and the Atlanta hosting committee, who worked tirelessly to ensure a smooth and successful event. Kenny ensured that we were all identifiable throughout the city of Atlanta that weekend with our Finbarr's logo'd shirts and caps. A few Finbarr's rascals showed up from all over North America to relive their glory days of Finbarr's "rascalism."

Notable among this group was the famous "Like-a-Bull" (aka Likeabull), whose real-name identity can be found in Finbarr's historical records of boys who were thorns in the flesh of Finbarr's administrators.

A quick search among the insiders of the old Finbarr's era revealed the real identity of Patrick Efiom, who is now Colonel Patrick Efiom, serving in the US Army Reserve. His case proved that rascalism reformed is professionalism achieved. Likabu kept everything lively and entertaining throughout the reunion. He told hilarious stories that kept everyone in stitches of laughter. He also led the group in singing several of the old Finbarr's football fight songs. The songs came in handy during the novelty soccer match against the Atlanta Green Eagles. Several spouses were also in attendance to share in the celebration of the glory days of Finbarr's College. Later in the evening on Saturday, Sept. 1, the dance floor of the hotel got polished with shoe polish with repeated sliding of dancers' shoes. Many previously under-utilized leg muscles got stretched again by body gyrations in response to rhythmic calls of the loud speaker of the DJ. Knees long used for leisurely walking got tested on the dance floor. The knees held up well under the watchful eyes of the several physicians among the Boys in attendance. Dr. David Toks Gbadebo was particularly concerned about the quickening pace of the dancers' hearts. Fortunately, there was no cardiac emergency throughout the dance sessions. The photos that follow tell only a small part of the full story. The boys danced the night away, not missing any musical beats, as if they were trying to make up for the lost opportunity of the Finbarr's days of "bone-to-bone" dancing in the all-boys school.

The highlight of the three-day reunion was the novelty soccer match between the SFC Old Boys and the Atlanta Green Eagles, a well-regarded soccer club in Atlanta metro. On the SFC side were three of the best players that ever played for Saint Finbarr's in her glory days of soccer prowess in Nigeria. Their rusted skills got revived, if only in two-to-three-minute spurts. Dribbling and tackling skills that had been shelved for decades were brought back down to the playing level to be revalidated. It was like opening a can of worms. We had never seen so many Finbarrians pleading for substitutes (for themselves) from the sideline. Stephen Keshi, a former Finbarr's player, who went on to coach the Nigerian Green Eagles national team, telephoned during the match and wasn't pleased with how the Boys were doing. His words of encouragement and hints of brilliance were not enough to rescue the day. The Boys could muster only one goal against their opponents, who scored three goals in quick succession. Of course, the coach of the SFC side, Kenny Kuku, blamed the loss on a biased referee. He must have been recollecting a quote (attributed to the Duke of Edinburgh) found in Father Slattery's autobiography, which says, "Football is as good as its referee. A bad referee can spoil soccer." Professor Badiru also participated in the novelty soccer match, where he introduced a new principle of the

Physics of Soccer - - - "avoid the ball." In the end, the victors and vanquished got together to celebrate the friendly match. It is a wonderful football world, after all.

Backed by their wives, as usual, the happy boys lined up (or, squatted) for a memorable group photo. The wives of Finbarr's Boys have always been staunchly supportive of the Finbarr's activities of the Boys. The annual Reunion gatherings and the 2016 group travel to Fermoy, Ireland for Father Slattery's posthumous birthday celebration are cogent examples of the togetherness of the Boys and the Wives.

A lot of literary history exists about the past activities of SFCOBA. Under the leadership and coordination of Mr. Segun Ajanlekoko, the Finbarrian Newsletter was published for several years by the national body of SFCOBA in Lagos. Printed archival copies still exist in the possession of many SFCOBA members. Of particular interest is the 1996 issue, which celebrated Finbarr's fortieth anniversary (1956 – 1996).

Reverend Father Slattery's journey home was literally back to his home country of Ireland and response to the call of the Lord.

This chapter gives an account of how SFCOBA tried unsuccessfully to bring Father Slattery back to Nigeria. He had wanted to return to Nigeria to die. All efforts to convince the Catholic Mission to send him back to Nigeria in his final days failed.

Segun Ajanlekoko, Yinka Bashorun, and I visited Father at his Maryland (Lagos mainland) residence on his brief return to Nigeria around 1998. When he was sent back to Ireland by the Church, he very much wanted us to visit him in his retirement home in Cork, Ireland. That visit never materialized due to logistical constraints. But we continued to communicate with him by phone and mail. That gladdened his heart until his death.

This following narrative provides a documentation of Mr. Segun Ajanleko's last meeting with Father Slattery. It shows, in retrospect, what could have been a befitting grand finale of the exit of the man called Father Slattery from mother Earth in Nigeria, but it was not to be.

While in office as President of SFCOBA, Segun made it a point of duty on a weekly basis to visit Father Slattery at his St. Denis

Catholic Church Home, to exchange words as well sought his guidance on matters that concerned the school, (our Alma Mater) SFCOBA, Nigeria as a nation, life in general, and, indeed, Segun's own private enterprises.

It was on one such occasion that Segun posed the question where he would like to be buried, if in accordance with his wish he died in Nigeria. He told Segun that he would like to be buried in St. Finbarr's school compound. Segun quickly responded by asking him where in particular. He replied by saying that it should be inside the retirement home that was being built for him by the SFCOBA inside the school compound.

Segun further asked him which particular spot. He then got up and asked Segun to drive him to the school compound. There and then he pointed to a spot near to his prayer room. Segun conveyed this message to the generality of the Old Boys. Thereafter, it became a project, which all Finbarrians both old and young directed all their energies to ensure would happen and be successful.

Unfortunately, after his 80th birthday in February 29, 1996, Father Slattery was asked to retire and was sent back to Cork in Ireland, where he began his ministry. But hope was not lost as it was on record that Father Slattery actually wrote his wish in his will. Segun, therefore, took it upon himself to regularly keep in touch with him on a weekly basis through telephone calls and whenever he traveled abroad, especially to Britain, he ensured that he had daily conversation with him from London.

On one occasion Segun decided to visit him in Ireland to be accompanied by the wife of one of our first-six member, Mrs. Beatrice Ozogolu, who Father Slattery had introduced to Segun as a lifesaver and whom Father Slattery told indicated had never, for once, failed to pay him a visit every month in Cork in Ireland. Her late husband was the First President of the SFCOBA. Unfortunately, the visit by Segun and Mrs. Ozogolu was not to be because Father Slattery fell ill and was hospitalized. Whenever Segun phoned him in Ireland, the discussion usually centered around Saint Finbarr's College, Saint Finbarr's Old Boys, plus of course, Segun's own family and his business. He was interested to know how the Old Boys were doing and whether they were contributing to the sustainability of the Association.

Segun recalled a famous statement by Father Slattery during one of such conversations. Father Slattery said, "Whoever contributes to the growth of his old association will never go in want; he shall be blessed in multiples for he has been faithful to the cause."

And then the end came in July 2003. Segun was in Europe and tried to phone Father Slattery as was customary, but he was informed by the Seminary that he was in the hospital in an Intensive Care Unit and he could not speak to Segun. Segun got back to Lagos on July 11, 2003 to receive a message from a Rev Father, an Ex-Finbarrian, who broke the news of the passing of Father Slattery, the great man and the paternal Father that we, his students, never had.

Two things I think are worth putting down for the sake of posterity, which emanated from Segun's discussion with Father Slattery while, so to speak, he was in exile in Ireland. The same topics were discussed with me by Father Slattery whenever I exchanged communication with him in the mid to late 1990s.

(i) The first one has to do with Father Slattery's abhorrence for what he considered a confinement and solitude in the Old Monastery in Cork. He was of the view that he did not belong there as most of the people who were there had gone senile and could not engage in meaningful discussions with him. Father Slattery, up to the end, had a very sharp brain and was very vibrant at his old age. And so he felt that birds of different feathers were flocking together in the monastery. He wanted to get out.

(ii) The second has to do with his fervent and uncompromised desire to come back to Nigeria to "live" out the rest of his life in Nigeria. SFCOBA developed various strategies toward the realization of this dream. One of the strategies was to ask

83

the Old Boys to write a letter requesting that Father Slattery should be released to us and assuring them in Ireland that he would be well taken care of by the Old Boys.

But it was not to be. The mission never caved in to the various repeated pleadings by the Old Boys. Meanwhile, the letter was never written, due to logistical obstacles, before the death of Father Slattery. It is a collective guilt of all the Old Boys that we had the opportunity, but we allowed the events out of our control to prevent delivering on the opportunity. Had we known that the end was near, we could have mounted a different mode of approach to get the letter written and delivered in person. So, our dear Reverend Father passed on, unsung (at that time), by those who benefited tremendously from his benevolence, his tutelage, his priesthood and his fatherly advice. If the letter had been written, it would have been another documentary evidence of the efforts made to bring Father Slattery back to Nigeria. This book and other similar efforts are designed to accomplish posthumous singing of the praises of Father Slattery.

Father Slattery has fulfilled his mission and would, no doubt, be working in the higher realms (the vineyard of the Father), where only those who have passed are granted the opportunity to belong. We, collectively, salute his great spirit. Live on, our dear Reverend Father Denis Joseph Slattery.

Watching us from above, we do hope that Father Slattery enjoyed the first-year anniversary celebration that was convened in his honor in 2004, under the leadership of Segun Ajanlekoko. The celebration was done in a grand style with ceremonial slaughtering of a cow.

Due to the special efforts and dedication of Mr. Bosede Odelusi and his UK SFCOBA, a posthumous celebration of Father Slattery's 100th Birthday took place in his home town of Fermoy, Ireland on 27-29 February 2016. The event was attended by former students of Saint Finbarr's College from various corners of the world. My wife and I were in attendance. Several wives also accompanied their husbands to the celebration. Father Slattery's nephew, Mr. Joe Slattery and his wife, Gene, generously hosted the Finbarr's group to a variety of Irish hospitality events. The photo journals in this chapter convey the breadth and depth of celebratory festivities.

Born on 29th February 1916 (a leap year), Father Slattery would have been 100 years old on 29th February 2016, although Father Slattery, himself, would have joked to be only 25 years old, going by the celebration of his actual birth date every four years.

As you can see now, I am forever linked to the legend of my times and learning at Saint Finbarr's College and the blessings of Reverend Father Denis Joseph Slattery.

So paved the way to the origin of the Rooster and the Hen. May the couple have many more years of happy union.

CHAPTER

8

Other Artistic Expressions

IN ADDITION TO MY drawing and painting pursuits, I have other artistic expressions, particularly in the literary arena. My love of writing was formed earlier on through voracious reading of novels. This is thanks largely to the accessible library holdings of the Yaba Public Library in Lagos, Nigeria in the 1960s and 1970s. I visited the library frequently and checked out American Western novels of the American cowboys. I loved the expressive writing styles of the Western authors. Reading the stories of the cowboys, sheriffs, and gun fighters were very satisfying. The stories were so vividly written that I could imagine and visualize every details of the terrains, the saloons, the corals, the trails, the horses, the saddles, the stirrups, the ranches, the outlaws, the marshals, the jails, the gunfights, the cattle drives, the guns, the saddles, the cabins, the streams, and so on. I could see the images so clearly in my mind as if I was standing right there on the sidelines; observing all the narratives in person. I checked out library books in rapid succession. My lingering passion for writing expressively today was formed in those early days.

Cowboy characters such as Scratchy Wilson (a jumpy and nervous gunfighter) and Hogan (in Hogan's Ways) still stand out in my memory even after all these years. The lyrics that I composed in 1971 based on what I read about the Ballad of a gunfighter still rings fresh in my memory. It goes as follows,

I am a young outlaw, way down from Yuma. I roam wild and free. I roam all over the West from Nevada to Wyoming. Although I am wanted with a prize on my head, no one can stop me because I am quick on the draw. Tonight, I am going to see my Doris. I will whistle our love song and her lips will be waiting. I am under her window. Come down, dear Doris. I heard a gunshot. I heard the Sheriff laughing while my life is ebbing. No longer will I roam wild and free because the girl I love has no need for an outlaw, but the gold that was offered for me.

I recited this composition admiringly again and again in my social circles of the early to mid-1970s. The expressiveness of the lyric continues to capture my literary imagination.

Now, I write technical books as well as recreational missives and monographs. I take delight in what I call miscellaneous writings. A selected collection is presented in this chapter.

Poems

Poem for my daughter, Abi:

ABI*lity*

Abi, I know you can do it;
Because you have abi-lity.
You are able and capable.
Your ability makes you the best.

Yes, you're the best.
Rain or shine, you're the best.
Top or down, you're the best.
Hill or valley, you're the best.
Sky or sea, you're the best.
Inside or out, you're the best.
Cherish the ability title;
And let the proud moment linger on.
You're Abi; the root of ability.
Yes, you can do it, Abi;
And you're the best.
Because; You're ABIlity.

Poem for my son, Ade

ADE

Ade!
Ade Badiru.
Adetokunboh Badiru.
A is for accomplishments.
A is for agility.
D is for dedication.
D is for determined.
E is for Exceptional.
E is for Expertise.
Yes, Ade is for all of the above and more.
Above all, Ade is for Excellence!
Gloat and glow in the triumph of the moment;
For more accolADEs are yet to come.
As the brightness of the sun never goes out;
Son, keep the candle of ADE burning brightly.

Poem about clouds

Above the Clouds at Dawn

The moon shineth still at dawn;
The blanket of darkness gently lifting;
To reveal the light of day to come.
Above the clouds we fly.

On a journey bridging two continents;
The bird of transport glides through the air;
Above the clouds at dawn.
What a pretty sight it is;
From my vantage point above the clouds.

Mine surpasseth a bird's eye view;
Flying where no bird dares fly;
The clouds rolleth though, like solid mountains they appear.
From here, I have the first glimpse of the day to come.

The end of the overnight journey is at hand;
Soon we'll burst through the clouds to meet the land.
Once again, with solid ground below and the sky and clouds above;
Like nature meant it to be.

Poem about possibilities

Beyond the Realm of Impossibility

I like making the impossible possible;
Bringing far away things nearer;

Converting gloom into bloom;
Turning mistakes into lessons;
Making good what is bad;

Churning challenges into deeds;
Doing what is said can't be done;
Finding glitter where only ruin prevails;

Marrying concepts apparently incompatible;
Cultivating that which appears barren;
Changing negative to positive;

Bringing mountains down to earth;
Turning impossibility into done;
Dealing in ways that transcend all others; because, I make it work.

Turning failure into success;
Yes, that's my way; because, I am beyond the realm of impossibility.

Poem about busy Bisi

Bisi like busy is Bisi the busy;
She is always busy.
Bisi wakes up early just to be busy;
Bisi wears an apron to keep herself busy;
Bisi wakes up before Grandpa to help him with his busy day;
Bisi likes going to school, where she can be her Bisi self; always busy.
Bisi loves going to festivals, where she likes rides, just to be busy.
Up and down Bisi goes on a ride, being busy again.
Bisi the busy; she is always busy.
Little Bisi is a Big competition for Grandpa's busy ways.
Bisi must be a busy bee.

Poem about early risers

Earley The Early Riser

Earley Early;
He is always early;
He gets up at the crack of dawn;
He does a million things before the sun rises;
He does more after the sun sets;
He is always on the move with more errands to run;
He rises to the occasion on each and every day;
From Mass to Mass he goes, amassing goodwill for all.
Earley Early is a model for all early risers.

Poem about feelings

Feelings that Linger

Honey, My dear, the tender feelings are meant to linger;
Even the passing of years cannot abate feelings that linger.
The special feeling will remain special.
The special moments form memories of a lifetime.
Let's not forget, what is promised will be delivered, for better for
worse;

It is an unwritten contract of feelings, feelings deep in the bowels
of the heart.
Patience is a virtue of love;
Tenderness is a virtue of caring.
Time and space are no barriers where determination of the heart
exists.
Keep your heart tender so that the feelings can linger.

Poem about love caution

Going Too Far and Too Fast

Caution on the love potion;

Going too far, too fast, too deep;
Heart racing faster than blood flows.

Already gone beyond farthest point than ever before;
Slow down and stop short of the milk and honey line.

Written as caution to youth in love.

Poem about the horror of earthquake

Heartquake from Earthquake

Nature's fever is Earthquake,
Which makes hearts quake and ache.
When earth shivers,
Everything in its path quivers,
Buildings tumble,
Bodies tremble,
Possessions crumble.
Gloom and doom befall;
And hearts pain and ache.

Shall we not appease the gods;
To stop the Earthquake, the Heartquake, and Heartache!

Poem about lollipops and popsicles

Sweet Lollipop, my Popsicle

My dear Sweet Lollipop, How sweet you are!
I admire you for;
Your sweet personality,
Your exquisite taste,
Your cool disposition,
Your gentle smile,
Your reassuring voice, and Your loving grace.

Thoughts of you send; Glow through my spine, Warmth through my veins, and Gladness through my heart.

What is love?
Love is admiration, Love is sharing, Love is respect, Love is trust, Love is confidence, Love is togetherness, Love is communication without words.
The way you look at me and I you, Sends only one unequivocal message, Sweet Lollipop.

My sweet Lollipop,
Beware of lust, the great scam of love.
Those who claim love at first sight only feel lust at first sight.

My sweet Lollipop, Ours is the genuine feeling of the heart, an everlasting state of the mind.

Let no stretch of time or distance, render the tender feeling asunder.

Poem to artistic expressions

Ode to the Arts of Cooking, Dancing, Painting, and Writing

Behold;
The dance of meat molecules in my pot;
The dance of my pen on paper;
The dance of my paintbrush on canvas;

Oh;
The tangle, twist, and tango of my feet on the dance floor;
It's all Arts to me.
Ingredients are to the recipe what paint hues are to the portrait;
Steps are to the dance what pen strokes are to the script;
And;
Of course, cooking, dancing, painting, and writing are, to me, the very existence.
Of what is life without The Arts?

Poem about rice

Ode to Rice

Rice, in my hot water, you rise magically.
You are the rice of my soul.
You are the rise of my day.
You are the apple of my eye.
When I see you, I salivate.
I live for you, you grow for me.
What a nice partnership that is!
You make me rise every morning;
You are the springboard of my day;
Each day, I rise to relish my rice;
The anchor of my recipe;
The root of my existence;
Without you, I am nothing but jelly;
I dream of you when I miss you on my plate;
Yes, you are my soul mate;
You are the very rice of my soul.
May you always rest in perfect harmony with my plate!

Poem about Summer months gone by

Passage of Summer

My Summer is gone;
April is history;
May left me before I knew it;
June is now distant memory;
Julia didn't stay long at all;
Augusta flashed through my memory.
Oh my goodness, my Summer is over;
All my Summer ladies left me; just like that; in a flash.

Poem about love thoughts

Thinking of You

I think of you.
I think of you, when I lay sleepless at night;
I think of you, when I hear the gentle rustle of Fall leaves;
I think of you, when I hear shadow's footsteps behind me;
I think of you, when I ring and the voice that answers is not the same;
I think of you, when I feel your parting hug;
I think of you, when I know you are gone but not far away;
I think of you, when I hear the bygone laughter we have shared;
I think of you, when I know thinking of you is refreshing;
I think of you, when I hear good humor and wonder if it's you;
I didn't realize the bond clean friendship can create until, I think of you;
I didn't know how it would feel until, I think of you;
I didn't realize what a world you were until, I think of you;
It's enough for us to know I think of you;
My dear, I think of you dearly.

Ọ̀eji Badiru

Poem about the passage of time

The Flight of Time – What is the speed and direction of Time?

Time flies; but it has no wings.
Time goes fast; but it has no speed.
Where has time gone? But it has no destination.
Time goes here and there; but it has no direction.
Time has no embodiment. It neither flies, walks, nor goes anywhere.
Yet, the passage of time is constant.

Poem about plane landing

Touchdown upon a plane's shadow

Up, up, above in the sky we journey;
Sailing on the sea of clouds;
With bird-like freedom rocking from side to side,
with each passing wave and gentle turbulence.

When we descend towards the earth;
Shadow raising in unison from the distance;
Closer to the plane the shadow comes.

With each passing stroke of jet engine, the shadow's size increases.
On the other side,
the king of stars shines ever so bright;
bringing home the shadow.

As the shadow and plane converge, pray we for save landing.
The ground rises up, so it seems.
Until, the shadow meets the plane.
Touchdown; and safe landing have we all.

Lyric about bodily desires

What the Body Desires

My heart says no; but my body says yes.
I will go with my body's desire this time.
Tell me you love me, even if you don't mean it.

Also of artistic interest are the 3-D concrete art molds that I make.
Below are photos of some of the favorite products of the concrete
art expressions.

It is appropriate to end this book's exposition with light-hearted jokes, specifically chicken jokes.

The Usual Chicken Jokes

"Why did the chicken cross the road?" "To get to the other side."

My own original twists to the usual:

"Why do some chicken have brown eggs?" "Because they go brownnosing in the dirt."

"Why did the chicken go West?" "To get away from Kentucky."

May the artistic inspiration be with all readers.

Printed in the United States
By Bookmasters